From Victim to Victor

The Power of God's Word to Transform Your Life

Apostle Prof. Livingstone David Covenant

WordTruth Press℠
(USA)

1st Edition published by WordTruth Press℠ in the United States (SAN: 920-2811). Find us on the web at WordTruthPress.com. You can contact WordTruth Press by:

- eMail: Info@WordTruthPress.com
- Phone: **404.919.WORD (9673).**

ISBN-13: 978-0-9852899-7-3

Library of Congress Control Number: 2013937883

Contents

Dedication

This book is dedicated to all who care about the soon return of Jesus Christ to establish His righteous kingdom on earth. To those who are seriously engaged in soul winning, depopulating the kingdom of Satan and populating the kingdom of our God. To all intercessors who are standing in the gap in their various countries. To all who are sincerely preaching the message of the CROSS. To all Christ-wounded soldiers and those who die in action defending the position of our king. To all who know the power and war of the tongue. To His Holiness, His Royal Excellency KING JESUS CHRIST, to use it to stretch and process the use of rightful words that bring positive results in the lives of His offspring on earth, who are waiting for His imminent return. And He has "made us kings and priest to our God; And we shall reign on the earth [through the proper use of our words]."(Rev.5:10, NKJV, emphasis added)

Acknowledgments

I want to use this opportunity to deeply appreciate Missionary Enefiok Umoren and his wife, fondly called "IMA-IMA-INTERNATIONAL," Pastor Ubenabasi, Pastor Udoh and pastor Bassy for their constant support, motivation, encouragement and timely advice and prompt response to my needs and their prayers that has become such a strong weapon to keep me in the mission field. I also appreciate Apostle Dr. Victor Akoh, Apostle Peter Ahiweh, and Evangelist Sam Oguneme for their constant willingness to give support in prayers, spiritual encouragement and ministry coverage whenever demanded by authorities in foreign nation Home Affairs.

I give special thanks to all my cruel and stubborn enemies and critics who are my role model, who have compelled and propelled me to stand for Jesus and wittingly become what God intended me to be. Every blow, every hit, every bite, motivated me and kept me going, and made me stronger and closer to the Lord.

Above all else, oh, a very special heart-felt attitude to my Supreme Commander, AIR-LAND-FIELD MARSHAL JESUS CHRIST – my shield, my glory and the one who lifts up my head. Through His ever abiding mercies I am not consumed. His compassion that never fails, surrounds me everywhere I go. So great is His faithfulness towards me in all nations where He sent me to go with His love, His heart, healing power and forgiveness. He is my portion and exceedingly great reward. In Him I hope, trust, live and move. He is the reason of my living. Everything else is His encouragement to serve Him.

Finally, my sweet, wonderful friend that I never have seen but believing that if Christ tarries, we may yet meet – The Rev. Randy Lariscy of WordTruth Press in Kennesaw, Georgia US. Apart from the editing, printing and publishing of this book, has painstakingly worked hand in hand with me, constructively criticising, commenting and asking questions to see that every word agrees with the doctrine of the word of God and that the book honours God the most. He is of the Evangelical block of faith but respecting my position as an Evangelical, Pentecostal and Charismatic. I tell you from my soul that we have a blended working relationship with revelations achieved from gleaning Boas' farm together. As the Lord lives, generations will salute the day he was born and kingdoms shall bow to God's working power and grace upon his life. Though today he may be but a few, tomorrow he shall emerge stronger and mighty in the mighty name of Yashua Ha-mashiah.

Introduction

A story is told of a certain vicar who used to visit the villages to share with them his wealth of knowledge and life experiences. He believed that this would help the people to live better lives and make good decisions in life. One day, as he came to one of the villages in the district, a young school boy prepared himself to have a faceoff with this old vicar. He took a butterfly and folded it in his hands, telling his peers that *"Today I will prove to this old guru that he knows nothing. I will meet him with my butterfly in my hand and ask him to tell me if it is alive or dead. If he says "Alive!" then I will pinch it to death. If he says dead, then I will open my hands and let it fly away and prove to him that he knows nothing."* So he went on his mission. He greeted him, *"Old vicar, welcome to my village, but sir please tell me this butterfly, inside my palm, is it dead or alive?"* The old vicar, with sober eyes fixed on his, stared him into silence and said, *"SON, THE CHOICE IS YOURS! Whatever you say to the butterfly inside your palm, it is your choice; it is up to you alone."*

The point which I am trying to communicate in this book has to do with choices. Every man's life revolves around his or her choices. Hence I put it this way, *"You are your choice and your choice is you."* Just as humans are said to be animals of habits, even so they are animals of choices. Your life results, on daily basis, are the outcome of your choices. Your tomorrow is at the mercy of today's choices. Choices are strong, propelling, determining parameters of your life. The habits you exhibit bear the fruits of your choices.

Choices are like well selected economic trees; you carefully choose which one to grow in an orchard. You borrow or buy as many as you can pick that have won your palette. You take them to your orchard and plant them, water them every day, protect the orchard, weed it and even add fertilizer. After about three years, they start regularly bearing fruits for you. Before you start trading or selling them to others, you are the first to taste of your labour before counting your gains.

When you look closely on the palaver of the fall of man, it all hinges on personal choices. Though in their immediate environment (*Eden of God*) choices were few with slim chances of escape, yet by their responsibility they gave Satan a vote, and permitted him to lead them astray. The devil became their tutor who taught them what to believe and how to believe it - what to say and how to say it. Man therefore by his volitional choice (*power of personal will*) was deceived (*the woman*), and became abjectly disobedient (*the man*). From one simple command, mankind fell into a stronghold:

- From simple order to a yoke of death and destruction
- From simple words of truth to deception, lies, spiritual deafness and blindness
- From glory to grass
- From life to death
- From provision, protection and preservation to the bush, to want and despair
- From health to sickness and disease
- From happiness to sorrows and endless progressing with difficulty, trying hard every day under difficulties and unprofitable hard labour
- From light to darkness
- From inheritance to poverty
- From a lasting environment and citizenship to depravity and deprecation, and wandering
- From a loving caring Master to a rebel

The fall of man has not ended with Adam and Eve's story in the Eden of God - it is ongoing. Daily, many are falling like their ancestors, Adam and Eve, and waylaying in the damaging consequences. They claim to live by faith when, actually, they are living by chance and fatalism.

Would we now blame God for creating man as a free moral agent? The answer is an emphatic *"No!"* In Genesis, the book of the Beginning, the Bible says:

> *26 Then God said, "Let Us make man in Our image, according to Our likeness; let them have dominion over the fish of the sea, over the birds of the air, and over the cattle, over all the earth and over every creeping thing*

that creeps on the earth." 27 So God created man in His own image; in the image of God He created him; male and female He created them. 28 Then God blessed them, and God said to them, "Be fruitful and multiply; fill the earth and subdue it; have dominion over the fish of the sea, over the birds of the air, and over every living thing that moves on the earth." (Genesis 1:26-28, NKJV)

Twice the word *Dominion* is mention here. In plain English, the word dominion can be traced from the word *domicile* which speaks of where a person lives. Spiritually, and in natural life, there is a place or thing where one chooses to dwell in, on or upon. Mr. Andrew, in his discourse, dwells much on how to stand for our rights. Where you dwell is where you can exercise authority; it is the place where you can speak freely.

Next is the word *Domiciliary*. This is a kind of habitual activity that can take place in one's home. Dr Emechebe has been personally visiting with the Ndukaya's to offer them medical care because they are more accepting of his services at home than they are in the clinic. Both the doctor and this family have something in common to discuss. The doctor, in his part, has a place to show his expertise and speaks to them about it so as to keep them in good health.

Next is the word *Dominant*. This expresses how powerful, how important and noticeable is a thing, place or person. Macbird manufacturing firm has achieved a dominant position in the world market. Because of their experience, they can talk about their success and how to keep the tempo. For every person there is a place of prominence to attend. Tailor your words according to what you want to achieve in the global hall of fame.

Next is the word *Dominate*. This means to control, to have great influence over someone or something. It may be in a pleasant or unpleasant way. James speaks significantly in meetings but does not dominate the meetings. Amos' progress has become the most obvious thing in the society that every company seeks his wisdom.

Now we move to the word *Dominion*. This word speaks about having authority to rule over people or places. It indicates how one can affect changes in the way things go, in how things should be, and in how people should respond to orders and duty. In the Bible it has to do with affecting a change in someone, something or someplace. Prophetically this could only be done by the use of spoken words of faith from the pure heart of a person who has died to self and lives for Christ Jesus. Hence what you will be studying in this writing has to do with your ability to make the best use of words to influence your future and maximise your outcome in life.

Let us examine another scripture that has a bearing on your life choices:

> 26 *"Behold, I set before you today a blessing and a curse:*
> 27 *the blessing, if you obey the commandments of the*
> *Lord your God which I command you today.*
> *(Deuteronomy 11:26-27, NKJV)*

God set before His people the choice of receiving a blessing or a curse. If you choose to obey God's words and remain separated totally from sin and Satan and all forms of evil – including those of your surrounding nation or nations where you visit or stay – then God's blessing will come and overtake you (cf.Deut.28:1-14). On the other hand, if you choose to conform to the ways of the ungodly, God's curse will come upon you and overtake you (cf.Deut.28:15-68).

Do you take the word of the Lord seriously? All too often people who profess to be the *born-again* turn out to be the *born against* by freely and comfortingly adopting the ways of unbelievers in words, lifestyle, and business methods. Such people risk falling spirituality under God's curse while they fix the blame on the devil and other people.

We even have wicked demolishers amongst Christians and pastors today. Yes, expert dubious demolishers using their tongue as they would a bulldozer. They freely jump into worship places, lifting up their hands to sing to God yet attract His curse. When they demolish the faith of ministers, friends, families and dignitaries they fan themselves as having done God a favour. These expert demolishers graduated from the *Statehouse University Of It Does Not Matter* with PhDs (*pull him/her down sincerely, first class honours*) with demonic impunity, who cares, or it does not matter. To the professor demolisher emeritus, it does not matter, but with God, *everything* matters. If you are under this curse, though your hand may join with God's hand, God cannot be mocked. That which a man sows, the same he will reap (Gal.6:7; Oba. 1:15). As you have done, it will return back upon your head. For a man that goes to the bush and gathers firewood containing ants inside, upon reaching home, if the lizards invite him for friendship, he should not be angry.

Words are like seeds. As you speak them on yourself or on someone or someplace, be prepared! You are a wonderful farmer busy sowing and growing your crops. Why not make them soft, simple and grace-filled? For one day, without remembrance, you will be made to eat them. The words you speak today, whether good or bad, tomorrow, you will reap and eat them to the full. Why destroy tomorrow today by what you choose to speak or say? That you have a colourful, big, round mouth does not mean you have the right to vent it in any way you desire. If you know it is not the right thing to say, then hold your tongue and hum inside, *"God be merciful on me, be merciful on me!"*

To bring this introduction to a close, let us consider:

10 Humble yourselves in the sight of the Lord, and He will lift you up. 11 Do not speak evil of one another, brethren. He who speaks evil of a brother and judges his brother, speaks evil of the law and judges the law. But if you judge the law, you are not a doer of the law but a judge. 12 There is one Lawgiver, who is able to save and to destroy. Who are you to judge another? (James 4:10-12, NKJV)

The principles here apply to everyone. When you condemn yourself more than enough, you turn around and start doing the same to others. You do not speak ill of another human being until you have done so to yourself. It is very palatable; your mind now tells you to take the hurt you feel and give it to others. If no one insults you, do not insult yourself. If you enjoy insulting yourself do not insult others. Start with yourself to use your mouth to speak words of life and not death. You are what you speak.

What you speak also exposes what is inside you. So say to yourself and to others what God has already said to you. He desires to bless you and not to curse. His words are His factory to create life and better things in life. As He is in heaven, so should you be now on earth to become fit for heaven. And remember:

31 What then shall we say to these things? If God is for us, who can be against us? 32 He who did not spare His own Son, but delivered Him up for us all, how shall He not with Him also freely give us all things? 33 Who shall bring a charge against God's elect? It is God who justifies. 34 Who is he who condemns? It is Christ who died, and furthermore is also risen, who is even at the right hand of God, who also makes intercession for us. 35 Who shall separate us from the love of Christ? Shall tribulation, or distress, or persecution, or famine, or nakedness, or peril, or sword? (Romans 8:31-35, NKJV)

If God is on our side, who is there to appear against us? No one can, except your own rough-edge mouth. Who is the one who condemns? Even the devil and men cannot, but you can with your uncontrolled mouth. Who will separate us from the love of Christ? The cruelty of hatred and venoms of hell cannot, but you can with your own graveyard mouth. It is far better go to the clinic now before you start spreading the contagious evil of your tongue.

As we move into the main dining table, close your eyes and pray these prayers:

- Dear Lord, by the revelation of your mercy. Open my eyes through the pages of this book to see the wondrous things you have in store for me in the name of Jesus Christ.
- Holy Spirit, as I read through this book, lead me to a higher level of life.
- Father, use these inspired writings birthed by Your Spirit to sow the grain seed of your truth into my life

and water it by the water of the Holy Spirit to intoxicate me into a breakthrough of kingdom life.

Chapter One

The Power of the Tongue

20 A man's stomach shall be satisfied from the fruit of his mouth; From the produce of his lips he shall be filled. 21 Death and life are in the power of the tongue, And those who love it will eat its fruit. (Proverbs 18:20-21, NKJV)

A man will be satisfied with good by the fruit of his mouth, And the recompense of a man's hands will be rendered to him. (Proverbs 12:14, NKJV)

A man shall eat well by the fruit of his mouth, But the soul of the unfaithful feeds on violence. (Proverbs 13:2, NKJV)

2 A man shall eat well by the fruit of his mouth, But the soul of the unfaithful feeds on violence. 3 He who guards his mouth preserves his life, But he who opens wide his lips shall have destruction ... 5 A righteous man hates lying, But a wicked man is loathsome and comes to shame. (Proverbs 13:2-3,5, NKJV)

You have tested my heart; You have visited me in the night; You have tried me and have found nothing; I have purposed that my mouth shall not transgress. (Psalm 17:3, NKJV)

26 It is good that one should hope and wait quietly For the salvation of the Lord ... 28 Let him sit alone and keep silent, Because God has laid it on him; 29 Let him put his mouth in the dust—There may yet be hope. (Lamentations 3:26,28-29, NKJV)

Let us pick out few things to reflect upon in the scriptures quoted above. Whatever may be the *"fruit of your mouth"* (Proverbs 18:20, NKJV) will become the satisfaction of your stomach. You say, *"How can this be when words are neither solid nor liquid?"* This is not literally spoken but figuratively; yet in some ways could be taken literally. The revelation here is that your stomach is the storage of your life; whatever you speak will be eaten by you until the storage of your life is filled. Then digestion and circulation to the whole body system proceeds from there.

Your whole life course will be satiated and saturated with the final outcome or harvest of whatever you voice - whether good or bad words, speeches or utterances. James in his writing took time lamenting over the wicked havoc the tongue can create when not sanctified by the word of the Lord through the regeneration of the soul.

> *2 ... If anyone does not stumble in word, he is a perfect man, able also to bridle [tame] the whole body. 3 Indeed, we put bits in horses' mouths that they may obey us, and we turn their whole body. 4 Look also at ships: although they are so large and are driven by fierce winds, they are turned by a very small rudder wherever the pilot desires. 5 Even so the tongue is a little member and boasts great things. See how great a forest a little fire kindles! 6 And the tongue is a fire, a world of iniquity. The tongue is so set among our members that it defiles the whole body, and*

*sets on fire the course of nature; and it is set on fire by
hell. 7 For every kind of beast and bird, of reptile and
creature of the sea, is tamed and has been tamed by
mankind. 8 But no man can tame the tongue. It is an
unruly evil, full of deadly poison. 9 With it we bless our
God and Father, and with it we curse men [even our
children, spouses, siblings, neighbours, house use and
wards and dependents], who have been made in the
similitude [image] of God. 10 Out of the same mouth
proceed blessing and cursing. My brethren, these things
ought not to be so. 11 Does a spring send forth fresh
water and bitter from the same opening? 12 Can a fig
tree, my brethren, bear olives, or a grapevine bear figs?
Thus no spring yields both salt water and fresh [water].
(James 3:2-12, NKJV, emphasis mine)*

When a follower or a child makes a mistake or says
something carelessly, it only affects that person alone. But when
leaders and parents or Elders make mistakes and speak carelessly
using their position as a helmet of authority, it can affect even a
generation unborn. In 1 Kings 21:25-29, the Bible tells us that
King Ahab had done some foolish things and attracted the hot
judgment of a righteous God. When Ahab heard about it, he
expressed his repentance before God. God saw his remorse and
postponed (not cancelled) the judgment. He lifted the judgment
from Ahab to the days of his children. Also in Isaiah 39:1-8, King
Hezekiah made some serious blunders. As he was rebuked by the
prophet, Isaiah, he did not repent nor show remorse, but accepted
the verdict. God's judgment came down, not during Hezekiah's
days, but in the days of his children.

So Hezekiah said to Isaiah, "The word of the Lord which you have spoken is good!" For he said, "At least there will be peace and truth in my days." (Isaiah 39:8, NKJV)

If Hezekiah were living today and was confronted by his pastor, he might have said something like this: "*What the Lord has determined to do, my pastor, it is very good but what is that to me now? Let me enjoy peace in my days but my children could become eunuchs in their days.*" As Israel's king, Hezekiah was the spiritual leader of the nation. His foolish actions impacted not just himself, but a generation of people yet to come.

This is why some people suffer today; even though they are duly born again and do their best possible to please God, they abide daily in the bitter gall of life, eating the bread of sorrows and drinking the ashes of despair with no better sleep at night. Their night season has no songs because God's judgment on the sins of their fathers has fallen to their generation.

When God postpones a judgment, it is for reasons that may not be obvious to those who experience the consequences. The Amalekites fought Israel when she was vulnerably week and unfit for war, but four to five hundred years later God visited their children for total annihilation. The Bible says, **"Thus says the Lord of hosts: 'I will punish Amalek for what he did to Israel, how he ambushed him on the way when he came up from**

Egypt." *(1 Samuel 15:2, NKJV)* They were the descendants of Amalek who was the first to oppose God and the nation of Israel in the wilderness (Exodus 17:8-13). The children of Amalek are the full representation of all evil powers and opposition to God, His people, and to His truth.

What you do not understand yet blindly accept can enslave you. Jesus said, *"And you shall know the truth, and the truth shall make you free."* *(John 8:32, NKJV)* But when you know the truth personally and accept it freely, you break the chains that bind you. *"The thoughts [ideas, imaginations] of the wicked are an abomination to the Lord, But the words of the pure [rigidly righteous] are pleasant [words that contagiously distribute life, grace and faith]."* *(Proverbs 15:26, NKJV, emphasis mine)*

Jesus said:

> *17 Even so, every good tree bears good fruit, but a bad tree bears bad fruit. 18 A good tree cannot bear bad fruit, nor can a bad tree bear good fruit. 19 Every tree that does not bear good fruit is cut down and thrown into the fire. 20 Therefore by their fruits you will know them. (Matthew 7:17-20, NKJV)*

Jesus spoke of trees with personification (personified trees). He was simply talking of human beings. In the realm of the spirit, the trees represent people. He also revealed here two kinds of mentors and parents, leaders and tutors with two classrooms. The life and mind-moulders and the life and mind-demolishers. After their convocation, they go out to produce what was inducted into them. When a criminal trains someone, what kind of person will that fellow become? And when the rigidly righteous who know the value of souls and their destiny trains people, what kind of people do you think they will become? As the old saying goes, *"Like as a father, like the child."*

O generation of vipers, how can you, being evil, speak good things? For out of the abundance of the heart the mouth speaks. You are your words, and your words are you. What you say describes you and reveals the sort of person you are on the inside. For as you think, so you speak, and so you are. Your hearers who love your kind of speech and sayings are moulded and influenced by either the health or poison you offer. Take a cross-examination of your mouth. Is it an open sepulchre (grave) or a river of life? A good man out of the good treasure of his heart brings forth good things; similarly an evil man out of the evil treasure in his heart brings forth evil things. What you have inside is what you are and that is all you can give out. A baby in the mother's womb feeds from the mothers body. Many people are in the womb of their leaders, mentors and parent psychologically and spiritually. The daily spiritual food of the leaders, mentors and parents is the food served to the children. So take heed to the warning of our LORD:

36 But I say to you that for every idle word [lifeless, fruitless, unproductive, unprofitable, unwholesome, irrational, colloquial, acidic, soared and detestable] men may speak, they will give account of it in the day of judgment. 37 For by your words you will be justified, and by your words you will be condemned. (Matthew 12:36-37, NKJV, emphasis mine)

Consider how your mouth has expressed your inmost thoughts to others as you are praying to the LORD. If you ask for God's mighty hand to work in your life:

Oh God, thou arise and confront my confronters and everything that confronts me. May every tongue that rises against me today be condemned. May every evil verdict passed against me, even by my ancestors, that is working against my progress today by force and by fire die in the earthshaking name of Jesus Christ. Amen!

This is a very good prayer, is it not? But now take some time to be quiet and meditate on your words - what you say and how you say it. Could it be that your own evil words have caught you in a trap. As you are inviting God to arise, instead of confronting your confronters, He rather confronts your mouth, and renders judgment on your life. Everything can be affected, including your health. Your prayers in the earthshaking name and in the bulldozing name of Jesus is now bulldozing you and causing earthquakes, seaquakes and air quakes against you. To avoid this, take your mouth to a specialist hospital for thorough clinical attention (*an ordained ministry near you*) before your prayers can now fight a legitimate battle for your ultimate good. Count your teeth with your tongue while it is day for one day you will stand before the Giver of sound, speech, words and mouth, to give an account of what He gave you for His glory. Words have the power of life and death (Proverbs 18:21) but you used them as free purchase weapons to kill, mutilate, hamstring, defile, amputate, jail, and destroy both yourself and others bought by the expensive, precious blood of the Lamb of God that takes away the sin of the world. Such bread may be sweet, but be careful that it does not fill your mouth with gravel.

Chapter Two
Why We Make Bad Choices in Life

While concentrating on the choice of words, I also want to generally examine together with you why we make wrong choices in life and suffer the fatalism thereof. You have some realities that cannot be ignored. Once you were born and that was not your choice. That was the choice of two people who consented to live together and one day or night, noon or evening, perhaps morning, as they were making sports in the procreation studio, it attracted God to address Himself to them. He took water and blood and put it into the creation basin, covering it for nine months. Then one memorable day, God brought you forth.

As you began to identify with nature, two people told you, *"We are your Dad and Mum."* You have no choice but to believe and take them as such. God, being supreme over all, is responsible for making choices that govern most of the details of your life. That is why it is safer to leave most of your details to Him to handle for they are His ideas and choices. Just a few of the things He decides:

- Who should be your biological parents
- When you should be conceived in the womb

- When and where you are to be born
- Your skin colour and blood, your height, your sex, your physique and life dividends
- The pointing of your nose and the size of your eyeball
- Two ears to hear well the things of life, things that edify, things that honour Him most
- Two eyes to see properly, as He wills, things to do good and not evil, things for real life with meaning
- Two feet to run errant to His glory and prompt command, and to walk properly with balance to places of profit with Christ centred purpose
- Two hands to touch, feel, handle, grab, work well and romance adequately
- One mouth so that you speak correctly, impartially, for justice, against injustice, with love and not hate or prejudice, with faith not fear, with commendation not condemnation, with hope not panic, with good report not evil report, for life building, with life-lifting words, sound words and Christ-centred words in view of the rapture

The choice of the fatal fall of man was of your ancestors, Adam and Eve. Today it could be yours to die: spiritually (separation from God); physically (separation from the body and man); eternally (separation from God and man forever). If you choose to live carelessly, then you will also die carelessly. Agreeably, some unforeseen factors may happen beyond your control or prediction, but what of those that do lie within your control? You have a life to lead and live, a faith to maintain and a race to run to the end. The responsibility is entirely yours. That is why your are most responsible for the choices you make and become the first recipient of it consequences.

With the understanding that God has given you the ability and necessity to make choices throughout your life, let us examine some reasons why many people make mistakes:

1. An attempt to feel big or powerful

2. Creating and setting goals according to someone else's script for what it means to be happy, successful and worthy

3. Adopting the patterns of those we look up to, like teachers, pastors, mentors, mothers and father even our peers and spouse

4. A naughty desire inside saying, *"The devil be damned. I am going to do it so get out of my way or life. This is me, not you."*

5. Feeling that there is no other choice than to do it this way or as it is

6. Lack of concern if it going to turn out good or not or if it is going to be bad all the same; thinking, *"Even if I find no good coming out of what am doing, after all who cares? Who's business is it? Leave me alone and mind your own business."*

7. Simply not knowing what right steps to take and evaluating properly whether it is working or not; a method that, at best, produces a mediocre result without satisfaction

8. Lack of education and awareness, which makes bad choices into options; to some of us as we tend to learn what it is that we really want

9. Peer pressure which, by far, has become a contributing factor when it comes to making life-changing choices; pressure which comes from so many sources like family, friends, fellowships and the society

10. Our perception of what we need to do to survive

11. Grasping for what is considered as the best option at the moment: Later, when the outcome fails to meet expectation, we scream, *"Wow, this was wrong!"*

12. Lack of good information and knowledge in the present is a strong factor to making bad choices for the future: Proper inductive information reforms a man and shows him the way forward - the absence of it deforms the man and leaves him to trial and error: the *"It may be this or that, here or there, this way or that"* syndrome - blind robbing hands on the wall to locate the door. You could be electrocuted for you would not know when your hands had grabbed the charged or live wire. There is a sad story of a blind husband whom they told, *"Here is your wife."* In an attempt to romance her he press his fingers into her eyes.

13. Youthful zeal and inexperience

14. Our senses can trigger bad decision-making: We all are guilty of it and most often it leads to big things like jealousy, cheating and overindulging.

15. Past expediencies and memories of parental temperaments and turbulence: Things such as divorce, quarrelling, fighting, hot temper, short temper, easy

irritability, irresponsiveness, abuses, and abandonment can cloud one's vision, creating a sense of inadequacy, feeling undeserving and a lack of protection that can all trigger bad choices.

16. Inability to see the future: What may appear to be logical could turn out later to be the wrong idea.

17. Hanging out with the wrong crowd: When you get into trouble, those who seem to be your friends disappear. Meditate soberly on the Scripture: 17 Therefore, *"Come out from among them And be separate, says the Lord. Do not touch what is unclean [Do nothing with their rubbish, their unclean and filthy salad], And I will receive you [Then I will welcome you as honoured]. 18 I will be a Father to you, And you shall be My sons and daughters [dignified son or daughter, denotes intimacy],Says the Lord Almighty." (2 Corinthians 6:17-18, NKJV)* This is my explanation of the text; do not fail to read it in your Bible.

18. Lack of wisdom and patience: We are sometimes in too much of a hurry, in a rat-race with no time left to properly think things over again before concluding. We fail to even ask from others who could help us. Our emotions and feelings become our counsellors. We do not remember to ask until the trouble surfaces. A man's thinking or ideas, to him is excellence, but most often the outcome leads to a fearful traumata and regrets.

19. Depending rigidly on what works yesterday that no longer works now: When I was growing up as a child, my father's first bicycle was called *Heculyse*. You had to have long legs to ride it so that your legs would touch the ground firmly when you came to a stop; today we no longer use that kind of bike. Today's cycles have

modernised to suit the riding of both short and long-legged riders.

20. The doggedness to resist a change and good cogent ideas and counsel: Choosing instead to learn the hard way with the hope that the lessons taught by those rough-edged, cruel and harmful tutors will never be forgotten and at the end they shall emerge as the latest gurus in town. Some will baptise it or Christianise it by saying, *"After all Jesus learned obedience from what He suffered."* Such think that they are now the modern day Jesus. Be careful; take it easy and look before you leap. There are potholes, gallops and empty pits all around. You are not even sure of how healed and strong your bones are to carry you. Check well because most of those whom you think you are leaning on are like a broken tooth in the day of festival and a broken bone in the hour of calamity.

21. Choosing to keep God and His ideals off your routines: The head of the wicked and the nation that forgets God shall be turned into hell. Do not gamble your life on them.

22. Over dependency on others to control your life when you have already attained the age of accountability: No one should have arbitrary control over your life except you. This is different from being under leadership for you must be governable. Without true followership, there can be no true leadership. Readers today are leaders tomorrow, but the reader must have a guide. There is a difference between someone over-caring and protectively having control over you; and you taking charge of your life when you are above crawling. You alone are the first and authorised estate manager to run

your life. So break the chain and say thank you to them before care becomes bondage.

23. Hungrily seeking for a father or mother figure so you surrender your life as a sympathy package to predators.

24. An attitude that since life has rejected you then you must reject life: Sadness and moroseness is not the answer to life. Instead of your countenance frightening people with the heavy load on your head, place it on your shoulder. When it becomes too heavy, swing your shoulder to allow it to drop away and just keep going. If no one cares, there is still a STAR that shines at night when all the others stars disappear.

The big question of why we make wrong choices in life is a crucial one, not to be ignored. The main reason is because at a particular time in our lives it most probably felt like the right thing to do. We do not possess the power of hindsight in the present. We live and make mistakes. We have all done it because we are often faced with situation that requires a choice. We know the right choice, but we make the wrong one. When we have made similar choices many times before – and it has never turned out well – why do we insist on doing it anyway? Many people make so many bad choices in their lives, more than they care to admit. They often regret those choices and wish they had a time machine; they would go back and make the right choice but *"Mr. And Mrs. who knows, it may work now?"* would not allow them. So they remain victims, but for how long should this be I ask you?

"Bon, Anderson, Jane, Honey, why did you do that?" is a question often asked by spouses, parents, and teachers at some point in their lives. The wisest man on the planet can sometimes make a bad choice. In life, it seems to come so easy to most people. In this day and age, everyone is so busy blaming each other for their own bad choices in life. None can claim perfection, we have all at one time or another made bad choices in life. As the Bible says, ***"for all have sinned and fall short of the glory of God." (Romans 3:23, NKJV)*** God concludes that all men are under sin – so that you are not taller than me, and I and not shorter than you. This verse carries with it great eternal truth. Just as the fall of man is on, so also is new life in Christ Jesus. Yet *"MAN"* repeatedly falls short of the glory of God; even the most ardent worshiper of God and the worst follower of Christ. Some are worse than can be told, yet the truth remains:

> ***9 If we confess our sins, He is faithful and just to forgive us our sins and to cleanse us from all unrighteousness. 10 If we say that we have not sinned, we make Him a liar, and His word is not in us. (1John 1:9-10, NKJV)***

Denying our guilt and falling short of God`s glory through our choices – including the choice of words that have put so many into trouble (*even death and imprisonment, divorce, family squabbles and communal and regional conflicts*) – we are deceiving ourselves and mocking God and not walking in the light even as He is in the light.

Most of what is considered as bad choices are genuine choices executed at the wrong time, in the wrong place, and with the wrong intention. Some acted to try and please people who are unable to understand them. Why Jesus wept over the city of Jerusalem was that the Israelites failed to understand who He was, the purpose of His coming, and that which would have brought the peace for which they were agitating. Rather they hated Him, rejected Him, and surrendered Him to the Romans to be killed. May God intervene to help us from the hands of expert destiny demolishers, who misinterpret us, misrepresent us, despise our good, and use it as weapons to kill us.

Having examined the causes of bad choices, let us now look at how to make good choices.

FROM VICTIM TO VICTOR

Chapter Three
Choosing to Make the Right Choices

No one will live your life for you. No, you must be the architect of your life. In any way you choose to go, you are the leader (*the object and subject*). Your choice comes as a desire with multiple choice options. The implementation (*your action*) results in decisions that now determine your destiny. If you speak like a fool and choose to be stupid, if you behave like a nobody and speak to buttress your stand, then that is up to you – that is your own cup of tea during breakfast which you fix to your taste. If, however, someone selects stupidity for you and wants you to accept and endorse it, then it shows that you were first stupid to see that offer as the best option for you. You have the right to say:

> *"NO, I am not stupid. I am not a timid JSS3 (grade 3 or kindergarten) boy or girl, man or woman, and I refuse it. I revolt against it with absolute agitation. I am a mighty man of valour, a man of the day for my generation, the delight of the Lord of hosts. I am highly favoured of the Lord and there is no reason for me to be what you think me to be.*

Whatever people say and want you to accept, it is at your disposal not theirs. Consider the word of the LORD:

*1 Do not fret because of evildoers, Nor be envious of the workers of iniquity. 2 For they shall soon be cut down like the grass, And wither as the green herb. 3 Trust in the Lord, and do good; Dwell in the land, and feed on His faithfulness. 4 Delight yourself also in the Lord, And He shall give you the desires of your heart. 5 Commit your way to the Lord, Trust also in Him, And He shall bring it to pass. 6 He shall bring forth your righteousness as the light, And your justice as the noonday. 7 Rest in the Lord, and wait patiently for Him; Do not fret because of him who prospers in his way, Because of the man who brings wicked schemes to pass. 8 Cease from anger, and forsake wrath; Do not fret—it only causes harm. 9 For evildoers shall be cut off; But those who wait on the Lord, They shall inherit the earth. 10 For yet a little while and the wicked shall be no more; Indeed, you will look carefully for his place, But it shall be no more. 11 But the meek shall inherit the earth, And shall delight themselves in the abundance of peace.
(Psalm 37:1-11, NKJV)*

Beginning from today, be persuaded to be patient and have confidence in God no matter what happens. Speak from that confidence. The life of a true child of God is a believing trust in the Lord, and diligent care to serve Him according to His will. It is not trusting God, but tempting Him, if we do not remain conscious of our duty to Him. A man's life consists not in abundance: *"Give me neither poverty nor riches—Feed me with the food allotted to me; 9 Lest I be full and deny You, And say, "Who is the Lord?" Or lest I be poor and steal, And profane the name of my God."*

(Proverbs 30:8-9, NKJV) God gives us more than we deserve, and it is enough that one is going to heaven.

To delight in God is as much a privilege as a duty. He has not promised to gratify the appetites of the body, and the humours of the fancy, but the desires of the renewed, sanctified soul. What is the desire in the heart of a good man (*the rigidly righteous*)? It is this: to know, and love, and serve God. Commit your way unto the Lord; roll your way (*all that troubles your mind*) upon the Lord. Cast your burden upon the Lord, the burden of all that keeps you awake at night crying, "*Lord why? Is there none that cares?*" We must roll it off ourselves, not afflicting and perplexing ourselves with thoughts about future events, but referring them instead to God. By prayer and praises, spread your case and all your cares before the Lord, and trust in Him. We must do our duty, and then leave the event with God. The promise is very sweet: He shall bring that to pass, whatever it is, which you have committed to Him and are fully persuaded that truly He is more than able and more than enough, trusting His ability and availability (2 Timothy 1:12).

As we grow in life, we are faced with situations that require a choice. We usually know the right choice but make the wrong one for many different reasons: fearing we may lose or hurt someone or firmly holding on to what we consider our best chance.

Your desire to please other people to your own disadvantage blinds you to the reality that the fear of man is cowardice that leads to hell (Rev.21:8). You do it because it is viewed as the popular or latest thing in town. Yes, it may be popular, but is it popular for you? The best and latest idea, car, home, subject or whatever, does not make it the best offer for you (ref. 1 Corinthians 6:12). Yes, all of the options may be good, but not all good things are good for you; if some are, find out the appropriate time, use and benefit plus its eternal values. Find out first what the right thing is for your unique kind of individual.

Come out from the crowd. Stand where God want you to stand in life and the choices you make should buttress just that. Say it, believe it, and go for it:

> *This is where God wants me to stand for the type of person I am so it does not matter who stands here with me. I am standing in my post and here choose to be a true soldier for my Maker and I refuse to be a bad example in His hands. I refuse to be a dead fish floating on the sea of life.*

Find out the best part of others that can propel you to become who you were meant to be. Study people to learn from them – not to become who they are for that would be a waste of time. You cannot be a carbon copy of the original, God forbid! When you have made the same wrong choice many times before and it has not turned out well, why not pause, meditate, ask questions, and talk it over with God for the revelation of what He wants you to do? Avoid making yourself a hen-peck for what never works well and will not work well in the future. You do not need a time machine to go back to those ugly choices you made before that you dare could admit. But realize that NOW is at your disposal to start making right choices.

The process is simple. Begin prioritizing or itemizing everything you wish to do in life for each stage of life: Between 12-20 years what, 20-30 what next, 30-50 where, and so forth. Out of ten crazy things you imagine, think about:

- What is it that could wait?
- What is it that could not wait?
- What is it that is most needed now?
- What is that thing that is very good and people are hustling for it or scrambling for it, but as for you, now, you can quietly do without it and nothing will spoil?

We are talking about making the right choices in life and continuing to make them until they become a part of you, your chief life-pattern or style. Psychologically speaking, all of life revolves around a chain of experimented actions to see which one will work, especially when we are talking about discovery. When you spot a real problem, you study the problem by placing many queries and come up with a suggestion that leads to an experiment. If it reveals a potential answer that will produce a solution, you take action. If the action seems fruitful enough to reject any doubt, it becomes a discovery. Then technology takes over to retain the discovery and turn it into goods and services for consumers to start making their choices. In this case, your ability to see that problem and experimenting how to solve it results in appealing option of choices for the consumers to evaluate, quantify, qualify and accept as a legitimate solution. You have shown yourself capable of providing a solution to an existing problem. But it is now in the hands of the consumers to decide which goods and services are in their best interest at any particular time in response to their felt needs.

In the marketplace, you provide various items for sale: bread, poison, tea, acid, butter and putty.[1] Someone is hungry but you are not there to tell him which item to choose. You have finished your part by producing these items and placing them out for consumers. It is the consumer's responsibility to study the goods to ascertain which will satisfy his hunger. If he chooses tea with acid as water, poison as soft drink, and putty as butter because they look alike, the outcome is his own, not yours. So are the words dished out to students, congregants, voters, children, and friends through many communication channels: radio, TV advertising, broadcasts, news dailies, telephone communication, and the internet.

Both God and Satan have many goods and services to satisfy man's needs, but they will not choose for you. By your permission they can offer you their goods and services through their registered and qualified agents, unregistered and unqualified agents; but they will not force it on you. The devil, as normal, will polish the pole, and make the bait to be wonderful with glittering strings. You own the responsibility of choice and the outcome is yours, not theirs – it is as simple as that.

An old gospel song says, *"God does not compel us to go against our will, He only makes us willing to go by His will."*[2] The devil, on the other hand, will not necessarily compel a man to go against his will unless the man gives the permission to do so.

Look at the word, *devil*; he says:

I am call devil because when you delve into my territory, what happens? I vile you. I morally reprehend your morality. I turn you into a nuisance, a bothersome annoying person and give you the ability to cause nausea. And they call me Satan because when you say the things that give me joy, I tantalize you or harass your life with persistent carping. And they call my demon because, when you enter my demeanor, I turn you into irreparable demurrage.

You can learn from this tale. The moment a man comes to him to seek for the kind of assistance God alone should provide, he has ways to compel that man against his divine instincts.

At other times, he does, at the moment the man comes to him to seek for the kind of assistance God alone should provide. The devil, having been with God and gaining aces to Him, knows many facts about God and man. When a man turns to him, that man is telling the devil, *"You see God is not enough; if He is, it is not for people like me. He is too feeble to handle my situation. In fact, the truth is that He hates me. He does not behave as if I exist or was His creature and I am dying of too many problems. So you help me and I will turn my worship to you."* The devil will examine him to see what a good catch he is to him and what belongs to God, if any, in the man. He will laugh at his ignorance and say, *"Welcome! From today you must not greet people on the road; you must look to the sky without bending, turning or looking down."* Then the devil will put some wicked instrument of possession in that man, that he cannot turn – neither looking down nor greeting people. After some time, the man will pay with his soul and that of his people. If, however, that man turns to God again in repentance and in full trust and adherence, knowing that *"My time, days and life at its best is in thy hands oh Lord, the shepherd and Presiding Elder of my faith; thy will is best for me. Therefore will I both wait and hope in you, for your compassion fails not; they are new every morning. Great is your faithfulness toward me and all of them that wait on you."* Humbly trust and obey, knowing in His time God will make all things beautiful. His delay is not a denial. He is only waiting on you that He may be gracious and show you His righteousness to make His way plain before you and make His countenance to shine on you.

Imitate Christ, not man, no matter how much they may possess or be acclaimed. Like you, every man has a dark spot that, if you know it, you will learn nothing from him. From men we study places, things and events from history past but should not dwell on it or on those things or events to become like those people. Yes, men being God's method to reach and govern other men, do exert some high level of influence on us – sometimes without them knowing the full extent of this influence. But you can only be yourself to arrive at the person you were created to be. From there you can contribute your quarter to the world at large and your immediate environment – even your family. While people, events, places or things including peers can influence us wrongfully or faithfully, knowingly or unknowingly, directly or not, you too should strive to influence your world in the rightful direction and create your footprint on the sand of time. While history wants to form around you, seek to develop it yourself in tangible ways for others to write and read.

Do not be too timid and squeamish about your actions. All of life is an experiment. The more noteworthy you become or discoveries you make, the more worthy experiments you can make. Second, study the risk, experiment, idea and wisdom thoroughly to get all the facts before experimenting. Millions are going through experimental living. Do not be the next casualty, for many still need you: your family, your church and God. That is why you are still breathing when the enemy thought that you were gone, creating an empty seat. Life is all about risk-taking, for sure, but study the action completely before jumping out of the plane without a parachute or free fall knowledge. Before imitating Tom Jones who jumped out of a jet plane into a Boeing 747, ask yourself:

- Is that for me to try?
- Is my life worth that?
- What am I aiming at in taking such blind chances?
- If I miss, is my time up to die?
- Has that anything to do with my life assignment?
- What better ways can I best make use of my life on earth than that?

Oh, look at Adam Ages:

We were sitting together in class during our primary school days. I was much brighter than him. But look at him now; he is a professor of Lost Destinies in the Cambridge University of Observers; and then what? What stops you Mr. Brighter from getting your PhD and becoming a professor of Irrational Comparative Living. Is that life all about earthly pursuits? Have you not been told or have you not seen professors who are now profane, characterized by profanity or cursing, grossly irreverent toward what is held to be sacred, not holy because of unconsecrated or impure or defiled mundane philosophy and end up as disturbing erosion and perpetual derailment? Have you not seen people with "Level 0 Jesus plus simple faith in God" who becomes life changers and history makers? Wake up and smell the coffee of God's cup for you.

The first man that taught the world Mathematics and Algebra – who was his lecturer and which school did he attend? The first person who discovered human surgery – who taught him? You need to ask yourself self-motivating, heart and soul challenging questions to wake the *Eagle* and *Dove* in you to start warming up to fly. Throw the windows open towards the East, not the South nor the North, so as to give yourself ample courage to launch out. When a dog bites a man, it is no longer news. It could only win time limited sympathy, sighing with many questions attached to check the modality and the how and why. But when a man, or woman like you bites Bingo (*the dog*), boy-o-boy that is headline news! Free media coverage without you paying for the news – Give it a trial.

Listen to me my good friend: I love you and am praying for you from the very depth of my soul. But listen, instead of you sitting day-in and day-out with the old prophet bones, celebrating with the leftover food on the table of Elijah, arguing about who is senior to the other - Ishmael or Isaac, deliberating on who is next to sit on the seat of Aaron and Moses and watch the movie of Eli`s death, think better thoughts on what you could do that the world could celebrate. Imagine what would spur your generation to salute your destiny. You are the first and only of your kind. You have no equivalent. There is the you that is in you whom you should accept and appreciate for the world to emulate and write your name on a tablet of stones. What God created you to be has not come into any human mind nor has it been seen before, so let them see it now. If God was walking along the street of ever green flowers and met someone like you, what would God say to someone like you? Get up now and start saying it to yourself; keep saying it, believe it and abide by it. Start a clean new slate.

One of the toughest lessons to learn, especially for those who live in the western world, is to admit that we can actually make bad choice in life. Some believe that their perspective alone can change their choices; in this way they practice the law of Murphy – which stipulates that *if anything is going to be good, let it be good, but if it`s going to be bad, well, we had better help it to go on and be bad*. Certainly, as one grows in developing good values, his righteous perspectives begin to affect his choices for your values determine how you foresee your future. Paul says:

When I was a child, I spoke as a child, I understood as a child, I thought as a child; but when I became a man, I put away childish things. (1 Corinthians 13:11, NKJV)

As you mature in wisdom and understanding, it affects the kind of ideas you have that produce genuine life results. Your choices will change and, at that time, your ideas become good business. This inevitably changes your choice of words. Lesser minds discourse *people* while greater minds discourse *ideas*. Where you belong among these two will foretell the landing space of your destiny.

Once you reach a goal, do you often find your objective distasteful? Look at this moment that you are working towards, a goal for quite some time. Peering through the windows, you smell a rose or the aroma of chicken soup from a neighbour's kitchen. Do you tear off the window hangings? Do you change your suit or possibly your soup to look like what you are smelling? You know what? When that happens, I tell you the wine in your mouth becomes saliva. Immediately, you swing into wishful thinking and daydreaming: how the daughter of the president of the most powerful nation of the world became your wife or how his son became your husband so that the whole wide world could cheer you up and start making melodies with your name. So sorry, for that is how the journey of lost focus begins. A wavering man should not think he will get anything from the Lord:

6 But let him ask in faith, with no doubting, for he who doubts is like a wave of the sea driven and tossed by the wind. 7 For let not that man suppose that he will receive anything from the Lord; 8 he is a double-minded man, unstable in all his ways. (James 1:6-8, NKJV)

A man with a lost focus has lost direction in life and has thrown his destiny's oil and pot of honey into another man's pot of soup. The rest of his earthly voyage will be called the "*lost, wasted years, Oh how foolish!*" He gradually becomes a doped or unfortunate version of his creational agenda, appalling fragments of an unpublished story. Before attempting to remove something from the roof top, first measure the distance to see whether it agrees with the length of hand before you jump; otherwise you find the world losing the aroma of your brain faculty. Inside your chemistry, within your mouth, buried in your tongue, deep inside your brain, oh, within the distance of your eyes, there is a daring gift this world needs. Please do not deny them that gift. Release it out and generations will salute the day you were born and bow to your grace and genius - your exceptional creative ability and dazzling skills in your field. Discover what you wish to become – that is *your vision* – and how you want to become that which you wish to become – that is *your life mission*. To maintain it without sidetracking is your goal. Staying on it with genuine resolve reveals your value. Your value system needs a secure anchor called integrity so that without a governor standing around you, on your own, you will make right decisions: God-honouring, life-changing, life-generating decisions. Again, personal moral values cannot be sustained without integrity:

- When you say one thing and mean another
- Say one thing and do another
- When you say things for the sake of trying to impress people without it having any impact on you
- When you preach what you can't practice

Boy, shut up your mouth – you are not born again (Cp. *"Now if anyone does not have the Spirit of Christ, he is not His." (Romans 8:9, NKJV)* If the spirit of Christ is not revealed in your mouth, and in your character, then do not waste time posing as a child of God. You are not. Your father is the devil and your citizenship is of a rebel, for when your father speaks, he speaks lies like you because he is the father of it (*of all liars, deceivers, gossipers, slanderers and whisperers that separate chief friends*). Having the Spirit of Christ means having a turn of mind in some degree like the mind that was in Christ Jesus, and is to be shown by a life and conversation suitable to His precepts and example.

Do you examine your objectives daily before embarking on what you intend to do and say? In your objectives to fulfill your goals, do you find any objective distasteful? Do you work towards a goal but find out that your motives do not agree with what you tell people and do not honour the Lord? At such times, be honest about what you do and why you do it to align your action with God`s plans for your life – knowing that it will directly lead to your destination.

What people think about you is supported by the deep meaning that they give to you and your leadership. You keep waiting for the answer that never comes. Your deepest desires remain unfulfilled, because they slip down in the background when it comes to your flourishing career. You are like a passenger who is alone on the way to a highly sought, impressive, appreciated, but gloomy and sad destination. Your life resembles a *hopeful* movie, but nobody watches it, and the movie theatre always remains empty – because it has action, but lacks romance. Your life is like a tree, the roots of which are anchored in people's hearts but fruits are never harvested. The Bible says that the fruit of the rigidly righteous is a tree of life and, visa vies, the wicked fruits are a tree of death.

You can determine the issue of a mutual trust if you often interact with people and only if you are spiritually fulfilled. If you possess the appropriate personal qualities, if you resemble those around you when it comes to mentality, honesty and commitment, they can get close to you and become increasingly willing to follow you. In order to exist in people's hearts, you must deeply anchor into their reality, values and feelings.

23 and be renewed in the spirit of your mind, 24 and that you put on the new man which was created according to God, in true righteousness and holiness. 25 Therefore, putting away lying, "Let each one of you speak truth with his neighbor," for we are members of one another. 26 "Be angry, and do not sin": do not let the sun go down on your wrath, 27 nor give place to the devil. 28 Let him who stole steal no longer, but rather let him labor, working with his hands what is good, that he may have something to give him who has need. 29 Let no corrupt word proceed out of your mouth, but what is good for necessary edification, that it may impart grace to the hearers. 30 And do not grieve the Holy Spirit of God, by whom you were sealed for the day of redemption. 31 Let all bitterness, wrath, anger, clamor, and evil speaking be put away from you, with all malice. 32 And be kind to one another, tenderhearted, forgiving one another, even as God in Christ forgave you. (Ephesians 4:23-32, NKJV)

1 Therefore be imitators of God as dear children. 2 And walk in love, as Christ also has loved us and given Himself for us, an offering and a sacrifice to God for a sweet-smelling aroma. (Ephesians 5:1,2, NKJV)

Let this mind be in you which was also in Christ Jesus. (Philippians 2:5, NKJV)

15 But if you bite and devour one another, beware lest you be consumed by one another! ... 25 If we live in the Spirit, let us also walk in the Spirit. 26 Let us not become conceited, provoking one another, envying one another. (Galatians 5:15,25,26, NKJV)

As His dear children, (*hoping that you are*), the same disposition and temper that was in Christ ought to be found in you

– in what you say to yourself and others; in the way you conduct yourself and carry out you daily functions. And it must be seen in your chains of relationships, accepting the limitations of humanity, and the voluntary nonuser of some of your cogent prerogatives throughout your earthly pilgrimage. Put on Christ's nature, heart and spirit toward fellow mankind, especially those of the household of faith. Establish a direct relationship between you and others – a full and peaceful integration in their inner universe and allow them a guest room in your universe. Time has a deep force, a strange power of appreciation and illustration of all the feelings and thoughts that you have about your future. And the time you spend with a dear, cheerful and lively person can provide you an answer to one of your basic questions of your existence: *"Who am I?"* When you stoop down to lift up someone, perhaps by your kind and graceful words or in response to their needs, you are equally lifting up yourself. But when you pull or run down a person, you have pulled and run down yourself. When you attend another persons` funeral, you prepare many friends for you own. Live and let me live. Is your heart right with me as my heart is right with you? As King David said, ***"I am for peace; But when I speak, they are for war." (Psalm 120:7, NKJV)***

Make this choice today and reap a bumper harvest tomorrow. Help others to make things right in their lives. Just as a painter transforms reality – giving the nature that he renders a streak of fondness, light, and tranquility – produce a positive and healthy change in somebody's life today. Give to others a new meaning, a new understanding, a new horizon, translated through a state of inner peace and harmony from the fountain of the new wine from Calvary's fountain. Work toward a total change in those you influence, bringing great inner satisfaction, a feeling of comfort, not only feeling better, but also feeling balanced in all respects. *"Brother, take me to the cross and point me to Jesus, Him crucified, and we will dwell there together for eternity."*

Look at your worker, office messenger, house help, relation of yours, or the fellow worshiper in your church who has been walking on grass, sleeping on dust, and drinking ashes as tea, bathing with tears – can he, through you, breathe a sigh of relief and feel refreshed as a child who is happily learning to walk, and suddenly becoming more lively, dynamic, vivacious? The bright side of his soul was reawakened to life. Oh, in this way the Scripture which says *"The memory of the righteous is blessed"* *(Proverbs 10:7, NKJV)* will be engraved in the marbles of your destiny. Like Mama Elizabeth Zacharias, your relatives will have a child in their old age from she who was said to be barren. *"For with God nothing will be impossible." (Luke 1:37, NKJV)* Am I hearing you say: *"Behold the maidservant [or manservant] of the Lord! Let it be to me according to your word. (Luke 1:38, NKJV)*?

From today, choose to contribute to spiritual humility, discipline, teaching, correction, and exhortation of yourself and humankind. People are relying on you alone for food from the Word. Choose to lead a soul from the spirit of arrogance, and spiritual independence. Choose to give a place for spiritually qualified seekers to be protected from the cool of the evil night; by so doing the Lord Himself will be to you a mighty river that cannot be crossed. There is no more stable investment available that you can profit your soul as much as good choices – including the good choices of ideas, values, integrity and words. Start now!

---

[1] *A dough-like mixture of whiting and boiled linseed oil; used especially to patch woodwork or secure panes of glass.*

[2] Harris, Thoro. *The Hornet Song.* Retrieved May 25, 2013 at http://www.hymnary.org/hymn/GQS1930/d206.

Chapter Four
Choices and Consequences

One of the wonderful gifts that the Lord gave the human race is *Free Moral Will*, the right to make your own choices or decisions. All choices set in motion the *Law of Cause and Effect*. All choices have consequences. For example, if you choose to ignore the speed limit signs, the consequence is a traffic fine or an accident that produces more problems – even death. And that is cause and effect.

Because of David's wrong choices, God's judgment had to play out. Let us look at the prophetic word spoken by Nathan the prophet to the King:

> 7 *"Thus says the Lord God of Israel: 'I anointed you king over Israel, and I delivered you from the hand of Saul. 8 I gave you your master's house and your master's wives into your keeping, and gave you the house of Israel and Judah. And if that had been too little, I also would have given you much more! 9 Why have you despised the commandment of the Lord, to do evil in His sight? You have killed Uriah the Hittite with the sword; you have taken his wife to be your wife, and have killed him with the sword of the people of Ammon. 10 Now therefore, the sword shall never depart from your house, because you have despised Me, and have taken the wife of Uriah the Hittite to be your wife.' 11 Thus says the Lord: 'Behold, I*

will raise up adversity against you from your own house; and I will take your wives before your eyes and give them to your neighbor, and he shall lie with your wives in the sight of this sun. 12 For you did it secretly, but I will do this thing before all Israel, before the sun.'" 13 So David said to Nathan, "I have sinned against the Lord." (2 Samuel 12:7-13, NKJV)

Absalom treason, secret rebellion and raping his father's wives publicly were simply a consequence of King David's wrong choices – even though he later confessed and repented.

After this it happened that Absalom provided himself with chariots and horses, and fifty men to run before him. 2 Now Absalom would rise early and stand beside the way to the gate. So it was, whenever anyone who had a lawsuit came to the king for a decision, that Absalom would call to him and say, "What city are you from?" And he would say, "Your servant is from such and such a tribe of Israel." 3 Then Absalom would say to him, "Look, your case is good and right; but there is no deputy of the king to hear you." 4 Moreover Absalom would say, "Oh, that I were made judge in the land, and everyone who has any suit or cause would come to me; then I would give him justice." 5 And so it was, whenever anyone came near to bow down to him, that he would put out his hand and take him and kiss him. 6 In this manner Absalom acted toward all Israel who came to the king for judgment. So Absalom stole the hearts of the men of Israel. (2 Samuel 15:1-6, NKJV)

A plan was then conceived to raise an army against King David.

7 Now it came to pass after forty years that Absalom said to the king, "Please, let me go to Hebron and pay the vow which I made to the Lord. 8 For your servant took a vow while I dwelt at Geshur in Syria, saying, 'If the Lord indeed brings me back to Jerusalem, then I will serve the Lord.'" 9 And the king said to him, "Go in peace." So he arose and went to Hebron. 10 Then Absalom sent spies throughout all the tribes of Israel, saying, "As soon as you hear the sound of the trumpet, then you shall say, 'Absalom reigns in Hebron!'" 11 And with Absalom went two hundred men invited from Jerusalem, and they went along innocently and did not know anything. 12 Then Absalom sent for Ahithophel the Gilonite, David's counselor, from his city—from Giloh—while he offered sacrifices. And the conspiracy grew strong, for the people with Absalom continually increased in number. (2 Samuel 15:7-12, NKJV)

David's first wrong choice was to have sex with another man's wife. The judgment came back on him in like manner.

21 And Ahithophel said to Absalom, "Go in to your father's concubines, whom he has left to keep the house; and all Israel will hear that you are abhorred by your father. Then the hands of all who are with you will be strong." 22 So they pitched a tent for Absalom on the top of the house, and Absalom went in to his father's concubines in the sight of all Israel. (2 Samuel 16:2-221, NKJV)

7 Do not be deceived, God is not mocked; for <u>whatever a man sows, that he will also reap</u>. 8 For he who sows to his flesh will of the flesh reap corruption... (Galatians 6:7-8, NKJV, emphasis mine)

The judgment of God was this: *"The sword shall never depart from your house." (2 Samuel 12:10, NKJV)* Absalom was formally anointed King. Then he appointed Amasa commander of his army and they crossed over the river Jordan in pursuit of his father.

> *24 Then David went to Mahanaim. And Absalom crossed over the Jordan, he and all the men of Israel with him. 25 And Absalom made Amasa captain of the army instead of Joab ... 26 So Israel and Absalom encamped in the land of Gilead. (2 Samuel 17:24-26, NKJV)*

David commanded the captains to have mercy on his son Absalom:

> *Now the king had commanded Joab, Abishai, and Ittai, saying, "Deal gently for my sake with the young man Absalom." And all the people heard when the king gave all the captains orders concerning Absalom. (2 Samuel 18:5, NKJV)*

Then we see Absalom's defeat:

> *6 So the people went out into the field of battle against Israel. And the battle was in the woods of Ephraim. 7 The people of Israel were overthrown there before the servants of David, and a great slaughter of twenty thousand took place there that day. 8 For the battle there was scattered over the face of the whole countryside, and the woods devoured more people that day than the sword devoured. (2 Samuel 18:6-8, NKJV)*

Finally, we see Absalom's death:

9 Then Absalom met the servants of David. Absalom rode on a mule. The mule went under the thick boughs of a great terebinth tree, and his head caught in the terebinth; so he was left hanging between heaven and earth. And the mule which was under him went on. 10 Now a certain man saw it and told Joab, and said, "I just saw Absalom hanging in a terebinth tree!" 11 So Joab said to the man who told him, "You just saw him! And why did you not strike him there to the ground? I would have given you ten shekels of silver and a belt." 12 But the man said to Joab, "Though I were to receive a thousand shekels of silver in my hand, I would not raise my hand against the king's son. For in our hearing the king commanded you and Abishai and Ittai, saying, 'Beware lest anyone touch the young man Absalom!' 13 Otherwise I would have dealt falsely against my own life. For there is nothing hidden from the king, and you yourself would have set yourself against me." 14 Then Joab said, "I cannot linger with you." And he took three spears in his hand and thrust them through Absalom's heart, while he was still alive in the midst of the terebinth tree. 15 And ten young men who bore Joab's armor surrounded Absalom, and struck and killed him. 16 So Joab blew the trumpet, and the people returned from pursuing Israel. For Joab held back the people. 17 And they took Absalom and cast him into a large pit in the woods, and laid a very large heap of stones over him. Then all Israel fled, everyone to his tent. (2 Sam 18:9-17, NKJV)

David's Lament: notice there is not one word of remorse about what set the judgment in motion.

Then the king was deeply moved, and went up to the chamber over the gate, and wept. And as he went, he said thus: "O my son Absalom—my son, my son Absalom—if only I had died in your place! O Absalom my son, my son!" (2 Samuel 18:33, NKJV)

At this critical moment, beloved, let us take a close examination into the matter of wrong choices and its fatalism from our elder-statesman, King David of Israel. My prayer for you today is that God, by His mercy, will deliver you from wrong choices.

It will amaze you to see that from the time you awoke out of bed and opened your eyes to see the morning of a new day, with a new breath of life, until the end of the day, just before you close your eyes for sleep, we face, wrestle, and make many foolish decisions. For example:

1. Should I get up now or sleep lightly for a short period of time?

2. Should I go to work or claim that I am somehow sick?

3. What should I wear for work – this red, blue, mix coloured dress; the black slacks and white blouse; or the white, pink trousers?

4. I think I am running late to school/the office/my business/my journey: should I ignore traffic lights/signs or slow down to stop?

5. Should I just pretend I did not hear my co-worker's snide remark, expression of contempt, or silly and irrational words? Or better still, should I retaliate with a meaner behaviour characterized by or indicative of a lack of generosity?

6. Should I care that I do my best at work/school/church/business/home or be content with just enough to get by?

7. Should I take my work, home, marriage, school assignments, delegated responsibility, or business seriously with deep concern or have an attitude "after all, it is mine – who cares?"

8. Should I spend a little bit of fun time with my friends, peers, girlfriend/ boyfriend, spouse and children or relax in front of the television or perhaps stretch my legs reading the papers and carefree story telling?

9. The list goes on and on ...

There are indeed a million and one decisions a day staring at everybody. To the greatest extent, some of the consequences of those decisions are of minor importance while the majority are of grave and lasting (even eternal) consequence.

Sometimes, though, the decisions are more complex and the consequences of the decisions more life-altering, such as in deciding the following:

- My children are not doing well at school so maybe I should give up my job so that I can train them in my home school?
- Honey, should we have another child or not because as you know we have no male or female child? Never mind that we already have eight children, sexes notwithstanding, with such slim income that some of them are in the hands of predators.
- Should I quit my job and look for another? The saying goes that a bird at hand is better than a million others in the forest. If you drop the one you have for another that is uncertain, the pursuit may send you into dubious activities.

Listen my friend. It is life-altering or crushing decisions that cause many decent people, who were once Christians and pastors like Saul, to resort to consulting mediums, horoscopes, crystal balls, and fortune tellers and fallacies. Many pastors today use satanic oil to do miracles (*magic*) and prophesying. What harlots use in drawing customers is now used in drawing members to places under the disguise of a church where godly morals/virtues are lost. Abominable practices have overtaken the alter of divine sacrifice. These are the ones that cause modern day "FAR TO SEE AND SAD TO SEE" (Pharisees [*self-righteous or sanctimonious fellows*] and Sadducees) to register Christ with their father's demon *Beelzebub*. Choose the path of right decision at all times and avoid the unfortunate consequence of wrong decisions.

But then, there are times when we are not sure, and decision-making becomes a dreadful, daunting task. See what the word of God has to say:

Where there is no counsel, the people fall; But in the multitude of counselors there is safety. (Proverbs 11:14, NKJV)

Without counsel, plans go awry, But in the multitude of counselors they are established. (Proverbs 15:22, NKJV)

For by wise counsel you will wage your own war, And in a multitude of counselors there is safety. (Proverbs 24:6)

In spite of Satan's parade in many quarters and spiritual declination (a condition inferior to an earlier historic Biblical condition; a gradual falling off from a better state such as happened in Eden; a downward slope or bending of the truth to a humanistic gospel), Oh, Lord God, arise and help – the Bride of Christ, by her appetite and longing for the flesh of Egypt, has gone into exile in Egypt and Babylon. Oh, Christ's Bride is lost inside a thick blanket, snoring with deep sleep in the cool air and sneezing in the Egyptian market place. Oh, she has become like Egyptian and Babylonian babies. This is the heart-wrenching condition abounding in every place today with religion taking over the world and demonic agents becoming pastors and emissaries. Notwithstanding, God still has reliable service men and women which the devil has not discovered nor established a highway

71

through their stomach to gain their heart. Look for them to help you. While you know not which way to follow, the Lord has placed me here to help you. At the end of this book you can find my contact information and you will be glad you did.

Never turn to some persons who can simply tell you what to do, or make those decisions for you. Perhaps then, you can be absolved of any blame when the decision does not turn out right:

> *13 Therefore my people have gone into captivity, Because they have no knowledge; Their honorable men are famished, And their multitude dried up with thirst. 14 Therefore Sheol [the grave] has enlarged itself And opened its mouth beyond measure; Their glory and their multitude and their pomp, And he who is jubilant, shall descend into it. (Isaiah 5:13-14, NKJV)*

If you want to enjoy divine communication, obey both what is written in the Word of God and what the Spirit of God is speaking to you. Cultivate the discipline of hearing, recognizing and obeying the voice of God now. If you do not know how to hear the voice of God when you are in serious need of it, you may be at the mercy of others who may not be sure themselves but are just bold to tell you something they conceive as what God is saying and they may mislead you. In the alternative, in dire need of the voice of God, you may resort to Saul faulty approach – patronizing the fortune-tellers contrary to the Word of God. And that will amount to opening your life to demonic operations.

The story of David's adultery with Bathsheba in 2 Sam.11:1-27 is a story that teaches us important lessons in decision-making. It is a sad, ugly story about infidelity and murder that, nevertheless, teaches us much about the consequences of wise and foolish decisions. Let us glean through it and allow the Holy Spirit to teach us some valuable, timeless truths for today, tomorrow and forever. I pray for you today that every pattern that ruins your forefathers and predecessors and is now targeting you to be destroyed by fire in the name of Jesus Christ.

"It happened in the spring of the year, at the time when kings go out to battle ... But David remained at Jerusalem." (2 Samuel 11:1, NKJV)

David, the King, should have gone to battle during that one time when he was supposed to provide leadership and inspiration to his men in the battlefield but he chose to stay back. This is the first, crucial decision that sent him towards the slippery ending that resulted in deaths, living under a curse, and being cursed by someone who supposed not to curse him: *"Hee, hee – come here, you idiot, a man of Satan!"* Tell me where does it measure up or size up Shimei with David (2 Samuel 16:7), a child of God and man of God? *Let the voice of the Lord like many waters and like thunder (Revelation 14:2) defeat every evil power of the land where you dwell and target them for destruction in Jesus Christ name.*

Having decided on vacation in the time of war, he was now faced with the next decision: how to spend his free time. Let me pause and ask you this question: of all the free time you have in a week, how do you use it? With whom do use it? To whose glory or shame do you use it? If Christ were to appear to you would you be bold, proud, happy or ashamed and sad for what He would have seen you doing? Yet, though not physically present, He is the silent guest in your place of abode or rest. It may be in your home, the beach, hotel or wherever you find yourself. David may have spent the first day or two quietly at his palace praying and studying the Bible and asking direction for the war. But one evening, perhaps when sleep was eluding him, he made another decision: let me enjoy the gentle, enticing breeze from my lofty palace roof top. Once there, oh the eyes traveled down the studio room: *"and from the roof he saw a woman bathing, and the woman was very beautiful to behold."* (2 Samuel 11:2, NKJV). Immediately, all the lights in the studio were turned on to allow a good view of the streaming videos. At once the mind signaled, *"Boy o-boy, this is it. What a beauty queen!"* From God's perspective, David should have turned away instead of lusting after Bathsheba. From the world's perspective, few would blame a man who stares at a beautiful woman, especially when she is bathing. But the world's values are usually in direct contradiction to God's word as we see in this terrible court judgment:

> *There was a case of rape brought to a local court. A girl was reported raped. Her father claimed he has so much money to send people to jail so he told his children, "If any one touches you, tell me." She reported to her father accordingly and the man was apprehended and arraigned before the court. The Magistrate asked him, "Sir, do know this young lady standing there?" "Yes, my lord, I know her." "How did you get to know her?" "My lord, I raped her and I took my time. I am praying that she will come my way again." The Magistrate was indignant saying, "Why have you done such a stupid thing?" "It wasn't a stupid game – she gave me an open invitation." Probing further, "How was it – written as a love letter or how?" "My lord, the way she dressed was the invitation." At this point, the court ordered the girl to go home, dress in same way, and come back to the court – which she did with police escort. When the court saw what she was wearing, some men screamed and said, "Can you please pass through my house tomorrow?" The Magistrate become furious and badly scolded the parent for allowing their child to go about setting a trap for men and ordered them to pay the rapist a sum of $20,000.00 for wasting his time and luring him to the girl. And the father complied.*

A married man might look away, and, perhaps, seek the company of his wife if she was around. Another man might simply move away. Eyes, ears, feelings and emotions are fast instruments in making choices and of drawing up conclusions.

David made yet another wrong decision, which ultimately sent him spiraling through the slippery slope that led to his own ruin and to those He so loved and lead!

The very next verse describes how David immediately, *"sent and inquired about the woman."* (2 Samuel 11:3, NKJV) He was told that the woman was a military wife, married to a soldier named Uriah. Another man might have stopped pursuing her at this point after finding out she is married – but is not *"He-Goat"* – David. He sent for her because the same spirit that fought his great grandfather, Judah – preventing him from giving Israel a king at the fourth generation – now engaged him in battle and defeated him shamefully just like his forefathers. The same poor decisions are made today by people great and small.

The consequence of their illicit affair is now impossible to reverse and difficult to deny as her husband was out to war – protecting the very Kingdom David was called by God to lead! The best thing David could have done was perhaps to own up (or *"'fess-up"* as we would say nowadays), and help support the child. However, he did the unthinkable: he orchestrated Uriah's (*Bathsheba's husband*) death in the battlefield when his plan to pin Bathsheba's pregnancy on Uriah failed. Why? David chose this charade because if it had become known to her husband and his commanders and Israel that he sought a vacation in the time of war

– only to impregnate his junior cadet's wife – it would amount to having the kingdom and the throne being taken away from him, and even forceful death. So, thought David, *"I will crush him and marry her as a widow."* When a dog bites a man, it evokes little more than sympathy. But when a man bites the dog and it dies, it becomes front page news. David plotted his demise with the help of Joab, the field commander, who agreed to place the innocent, willing defender, Uriah, in the most vulnerable position during a skirmish. Uriah was later fatally injured and died.

David, marked by excessive complacency or self-satisfaction, thought, *"Oh, now I am free and can get away with this murder because no one knows what has trespassed!"* He forgot that God knows. He sees the tiny ant that passes through an underground hole. You cannot hide from God, though you cover your sin that no man may know. There was an elderly man of God who has been in ministry for well over 66 years. He was happily married but had no children. During an annual convention of his church, all the pastors held a meeting with him and told him, *"Our Daddy, you have lead us so well for all these years and now you are getting old. We do not know when nor wish it to be so soon, but one day you will kick the bucket. Who will inherit your house? We have made an arrangement with a plummy G16 that in just a click she can be pregnant and give you a child or more. She shall be kept in another station. You can go there as part of a pastoral visit – nobody will catch the mark of the tires."* The man of God asked them, *"Are you through?"* They said, *"Yes."* He thanked them for their thoughtfulness then threw this question to them, which to date they have no answer. *"Have you people manufactured a thick blanket to cover God's eyes so that He will not see nor know what you want me to do? Then let's do it right here and now for I need a child!"* One by one they left in shame. I am praying for you today that you will let the finger of God scatter every evil counsel of Ahithophel assigned against you in the mighty name of Jesus Christ. Let Yashua Hamashua arise like a mighty warrior and confront all that want to quench your light from shining and bury your destiny abruptly in the earth quaking name of Jesus Christ.

God said to this backsliding general *(or pastor or deacon or Sunday school teacher, usher, or perhaps chorister or a governor or presidio)*: See I gave you all of Israel and Judah so you have absolutely no reason to be so greedy. If all this had been too little, I could have given you even more! David, all you needed to do was ask if you needed more and I could have given it you!

It did not stop there. Even after he confessed his sins, he was told that his son with Bathsheba will die. David decided to appeal His case before God. He fasted and prayed, hoping God would change His mind and let his son live, but to no avail. His son died on the seventh day of his fast. The law of divine retribution is as real as every other law. God will forgive you your jacks but you will not escape the consequences.

Beginning with the seemingly innocuous ones (*lacking intent or capacity to injure. Not causing disapproval*) to the downright sinister ones (*stemming from evil characteristics or forces; wicked or dishonourable*) that ultimately led first to Uriah's death, and his son's death, David could have stopped dead in his tracks and made the right choices. After his first look at Bathsheba, he could have looked away. After Bathsheba became pregnant, he could have confessed his sin and let Uriah live. He did not. There were many possible turning points after the first wrong decision (*he chose to stay home*), but he kept going down the path of wreckage. May you be delivered today from allowing your ship to suffer shipwreck from evil powers and influences at the manifestation of your glory in the healing name of Jesus Christ.

Brethren, we need to be very careful and be prayerful in making decisions. Decisions, even the seemingly innocent ones, have consequences and can lead to many regrets! If unsure of the next safe path, ask God to give you wisdom. In the early days at the Scripture Union we used to sing, "*My Lord knows the way through the wilderness all I have to do is to follow?*" Consider:

If any of you lacks wisdom, let him ask of God, who gives to all liberally and without reproach, and it will be given to him. (James 1:5, NKJV)

Sometimes all it takes is to be patient and take the time to assess the pros and cons of the various options. If I do A instead of B, what will happen? This process of decision-making is called the *sound-mind principle.* You must not be afraid to use your own mind. After all, Christians have been given a *"sound mind."* (2 Tim.1:7, NKJV). And the Apostle Paul declares, we have the *"mind of Christ."* (1 Corinthians 2:16, NKJV)

Second, we need to realize that making a wrong decision does not mean we have doomed ourselves to a life of failure, sin and misery! So you dropped out of school, but unless you are already debilitated with dementia[1]or alzheimer's,[2] is there anything to hard for the Lord? *"Behold, I am the Lord, the God of all flesh. Is there anything too hard for Me?"* (Jeremiah 32:27, NKJV) You can still go back to school and finish that diploma or degree. Though your first marriage ended in divorce, your second marriage need not end in the same way! Perhaps you lose your job or were fired with good reason. Have you messed up your life and been caught with red and purple hands? God says when we sin, we can repent and confess (*do what I call a complete 180 degree turn like a trailer driver negotiating a bend or turn*), and He promises to forgive and cleanse, so we can start over (1 John 1:9). It is not over yet. Do not give up! Do not give out! Do not give in! You, the cow that has no tail, the LORD God will drive the flies away for you. You, the one being mocked and laughed upon, hold on for the Lord is coming. He is coming soon – wait for Him and despair not. God can decide to close a door so as to open a far more better one.

We need to realize that some of our wrong decisions do have dire consequences. It does not help to play the victim and blame your self-imposed problems on someone else. David could have been belligerent with God (*a characteristic of an enemy or one eager to fight*) and blamed Bathsheba for seducing him. He finally made the right decision by owning up:

> *13 So David said to Nathan, "I have sinned against the Lord." And Nathan said to David, "The Lord also has put away your sin; you shall not die. 14 However, because by this deed you have given great occasion to the enemies of the Lord to blaspheme, the child also who is born to you shall surely die." (2 Samuel 12:13-14, NKJV)*

These verses imply that had David refused to acknowledge his sin, God would have taken his life. The rest of the Bible would have been so different! As soon as David confessed, God's forgiveness was immediate. He also allowed David and Bathsheba to stay together and give birth to the wisest person who has ever lived: Solomon. David, however, still had to suffer the immediate consequence of his sinful decisions – the death of his son. He fasted and prayed to spare his son, appealing to God's mercy, but to no avail. When God chooses not to change His mind, David did not throw a temper tantrum (*a display of bad temper*). He accepted his son's death gracefully, though painfully.

I have long suspected that aside from the fact that sin is an affront to God's holiness, it also pains Him. But I think it pains Him, because He knows that sin hurts and destroys us and those we love. Although God already took care of the penalty for sin, He does not keep us from suffering its painful consequences. If you steal, you will eventually get caught and perhaps be put to jail. If you cheat during an exam, there is a strong likelihood you will get caught, get suspended and even thrown out of school!

God desires for us to make right choices for, after all, He says: *"For I know the thoughts that I think toward you, says the Lord, thoughts of peace and not of evil, to give you a future and a hope."* (Jeremiah 29:11, NKJV). He has given us all we need to do and be righteous: the enabling power of His indwelling Spirit, His Word for instruction and direction, and His Church for support and encouragement. God does expect us to obey Him and come out a winner at all times.

Beloved, understand that sin is all about choices. Throughout history, men have used just about every conceivable excuse to justify sin in their lives. Consider the time at the foot of Mount Sinai — in the midst of Israel's wicked idolatry — when Aaron tried to justify his poor choice. When questioned about the calf he fashioned for the Israelites to worship at their request, he told Moses: *"And I said to them, 'Whoever has any gold, let them break it off.' So they gave it to me, and I cast it into the fire, and this calf came out."* (Exodus 32:24, NKJV) May God deliver us from pastors producing calves for us to worship as God. Such pastors develop religion with modernistic style and throw the historic biblical Christianity and the validity of the cross overboard.

Whether it is a one-time act, or a continually repeated sin that besets one, statements such as, *"The Devil made me do it,"* *"I had no choice,"* or *"I could not help myself"* have often been heard. Nevertheless, such thinking is foreign and contrary to the word of God. It is an indirect way of saying to God, *"You are not enough so I sought for what is more sufficient."*

The Bible teaches that sin is a matter of individual choice (reference Ezekiel 18). It begins with discerning good from evil (Heb. 5:14) and then refusing the evil and choosing the good (Isa.

7:15). A sure and consistent pattern for such thinking can be clearly established from the beginning of time.

Temptation is the birthplace of sin. We need to realize that we have not sinned until we give in to our temptations. This does not mean we should push the threshold of temptation to the maximum. Rather, we should know that even if we are tempted, we do not have to give in! We can still turn it around. We can still avoid sin. We need to simply say, "*NO!*" This is why the Spirit teaches us to:

> *Abstain from every form of evil. (1 Thessalonians 5:22, NKJV)*

> *Resist the devil and he will flee from you. (James 4:7b, NKJV)*

> *Flee sexual immorality. (1 Corinthians 6:18. NKJV)*

> *Abhor what is evil. Cling to what is good. (Romans 12:9, NKJV).*

We must acknowledge that even in the heat of temptation, as Satan is turning up the thermostat, we will choose to avoid sin by not giving any place to the devil (Eph. 4:27)!

Indeed, sin is all about choices. We make choices between right and wrong, good and evil, acceptable and unacceptable, pleasing and not pleasing, truth and error every day of our lives.

These choices make a difference in time and for eternity. Ultimately, the choice is between life and death. It is important to keep in mind: it is one thing to know right from wrong and another thing altogether to choose right over wrong. Ask yourself, *"What kind of choices am I making?"*

Finally, David's serious spiritual failures and God's subsequent judgment upon him, for the rest of his life, leave us with the following lessons to learn the rest of our lives:

1. This account of David's sin and the consequent tragedies in his personal and family life serves as a serious example and warning for the New Testament believer, not just for Israel.
2. David's experience demonstrates how far a person may fall when he or she turns away from God and the guidance of the Holy Spirit.
3. Although David repented of his sins and received God's forgiveness, God did not eliminate sin's consequences.
4. God did not condone nor excuse David's sins under the pretense that David was only human, that his sins were merely weaknesses or human failures, or that he, as king, could understandably resort to evil and cruelty.
5. The correct response to sin is to repent in all sincerity, to come before God that we might receive forgiveness, grace and mercy. (2 Samuel 12:13-14; Psalm 51; Hebrews 4:16; 7:25).

Instead of David leading his army into battle, as he done before, David stayed behind in Jerusalem. He developed a softness that soon led to his spiritual and moral collapse. His life and luxury as king bred self-confidence. At about this time, he ceases to be a man after God's heart and despises God and his word (Cf. 1Sam.13:14). David turned away from God's grace (Titus 2:11-14) stands as a timeless warning to believers: *"Therefore let him who thinks he stands take heed lest he fall."* (1 Corinthians 10:12, NKJV)

Even if we are faced with a tempting situation, the choice to turn away and avoid its consequences is still available — thus, rendering our foolish actions inexcusable. In truth, the examples are boundless. Sin is all about choices. James wrote:

> *12 Blessed is the man who endures temptation; for when he has been approved, he will receive the crown of life which the Lord has promised to those who love Him. 13 Let no one say when he is tempted, "I am tempted by God"; for God cannot be tempted by evil, nor does He Himself tempt anyone. 14 But each one is tempted when he is drawn away by his own desires and enticed. 15 Then, when desire has conceived, it gives birth to sin; and sin, when it is full-grown, brings forth death. (James 1:12-15, NKJV).*

From this passage, we can acknowledge some simple facts about sin, temptation and choices. Take heed therefore lest you fall. At this point close your eyes and pray these prayers against evil patterns. Please do not just say them as mantras – neither keep them as reading notes for in that sense you are just a joker. They are simple keys in your hands. Expand them to suit your needs. Spend at least five minute on each point:

- Every curse and pattern of careless indifference, affecting my destiny, break by fire, in the name of Jesus.
- Every virtue of my life that the enemy is sitting upon, come to me by fire, in the name of Jesus.
- Anything planted into my life to disgrace me, come out now, in the name of Jesus.
- O Lord, whenever I am stubborn, make me to surrender, in the name of Jesus.
- I release myself from the hand of destiny paralyzers, in Jesus name.
- Everything that bitterness has destroyed in my life, be restored by the resurrection power of God, in the name of Jesus.
- O Lord, repair every damage done to my life by evil patterns from argumentative spirit, in the name of Jesus
- You, the root cause of bad habits, together with your branches, die in the name of Jesus.

---

[1] *A mental deterioration of organic or functional origin.*

[2] A progressive form of pre-senile dementia that is similar to senile dementia except that is usually starts in the 40's or 50's. The first symptoms are impaired memory, followed by impaired thought and speech and, finally, to complete helplessness.

From Victim to Victor

Chapter Five
Choices and Your Responsibilities

20 A man's stomach shall be satisfied from the fruit of his mouth; From the produce of his lips he shall be filled. 21 Death and life are in the power of the tongue, And those who love it will eat its fruit. (Proverbs 18:20-21, NKJV)

From these verses we learn that the stomach (*or belly*) here is a reference to the inner man, also called the heart. The heart is often considered as the seat of the soul and affection where many thoughts, ideas, and words – whether negative or positive – are stored. What fills the heart brings satisfaction and inward peace or troubles and lack of peace. The word *produce* is the act of cultivating by growing, often involving improvements by means of agricultural techniques. Looking at the parable of the sower (Matthew 13:3-8,19-23; Luke 8:5-15), your life is a soil to be cultivated with whatever kind of word seed you choose that will be your benefit in full measure. The *produce* also denotes a process of becoming larger or longer or more numerous or more important. Hear this: your life today, tomorrow and for eternity hinges on your tongue. Many things daily go into you, but that which comes out through the agency of your mouth (tongue; words, thought and ideas verbalize) can destroy you. Your mouth is a *gate* for life or death, good or evil, blessing or curse that swings open by the gate keepers called *lips* and empowered by the little fire called *tongue*.

A false or injurious tongue can cause calamitous troubles, even death. Words have the power to contaminate, defile, and kill or reform, build, and restore. And God has entrusted to you the responsibility for what you allow inside your heart and what you allow to escape through your lips.

> *A man's stomach shall be satisfied from the fruit of his mouth; From the produce of his lips he shall be filled. (Proverbs 18:20, NKJV)*

Our comfort depends very much upon the testimony of our own consciences, for us or against us. The word **stomach** is used here also for the conscience. The human spirit is the centre of conscience and discernment, providing a window for God's light to bring spiritual understanding to your inner life (*the heart*) as in Proverbs 20:27. Now it is of great consequence to us whether the inner life will be satisfied, and with what it is filled. To the degree it is is filled with righteousness, accordingly, so will be our satisfaction and inward peace.

The testimony of our consciences will be for us, or against us, according to how we have governed our tongues. Growing in grace and maturity includes the ability to put your tongue inside a training camp of discipline. As the fruit of the mouth is good or bad, unto iniquity or unto righteousness, so is the character of the man and, consequently, the testimony of his conscience concerning him. "*We ought to take as great care about the words we speak as we do about the fruit of our trees or the increase of the earth, which we are to eat; for, according as they are wholesome or unwholesome, so will the pleasure or the pain be wherewith we shall be filled.*"[1]

Death and life are in the power of the tongue, And those who love it will eat its fruit. (Proverbs 18:20-21, NKJV)

A man may do a great deal of good, or a great deal of hurt, both to others and to himself, according to the use he makes of his tongue. Many have hastened their own deaths by a foul tongue, or the death of others by a false tongue. On the other hand, many have saved their own lives, or procured the comfort of it, by a prudent, gentle tongue, and saved the lives of others by a seasonable testimony or intercession for them. And, if by our words, we must be justified or condemned, death and life are, no doubt, in the power of the tongue. A concession given to mollify (*make more temperate, acceptable, or suitable by adding something else; moderate*) or placate (*cause to be more favourably inclined; to gain the good will*) has the tongue as its best meat, and its worst.

Your words will be judged by the affections with which they are spoken. He that not only speaks aright (*which a bad man may do to save his credit or please his company*) – but loves to speak so, speaks well of choice, and with delight, to him it will be life. He that not only speaks amiss (*which a good man may do through inadvertency*), but loves to speak so to him it will be death. As men love it, they shall eat the fruit of it.

If the words you speak spring from your stomach (*heart*), then what is the origin of those words? Consider God's word to the prophet Jeremiah:

> **9 Then the Lord put forth His hand and touched my mouth, and the Lord said to me: "Behold, I have put My words in your mouth. 10 See, I have this day set you over the nations and over the kingdoms, To root out and to pull down, To destroy and to throw down, To build and to plant." (Jeremiah 1:9-10, NKJV)**

So the question we need to ask ourselves is, "*Who put the words in my mouth that I speak daily to my situation and other people's conditions: the devil or God?*" Both have power to produce tangible results. The source of your words can come from:

- God, through His spirit, working and dwelling in us.
- Satan, through his spirit, working and dwelling in us.
- Men, through the relationships that bind us with them.

- Events, through what we see and how we see it, what we hear and how we hear it, what we feel or experience and how it affect us, what happens to those so dear to us and how it occurred.

What you will amount to in life, to a large extent, depends on what you say and believe. You are what you believe and no one, not even God, can change what you believe.. And your word defines you. Your eyes, ears, feeling, touch and smell contribute or forms our speaking and believing system. What your eyes see and ears hear are captured inside, digested slowly, progressively and spring up to your mouth to speak. A complainer does not win the war; rather, he eats his soul and becomes a prisoner of war (a P.O.W). God does not answer complaints and murmurings. He answers prayers that are in line with His purposes for your life. You are His idea and He is committed to that which is His in you. One of the songs we used to sing in those good days in Scripture Union is, "*I will dig a little deeper. Jesus words become sweeter. I will dig a little deeper, deeper yes.*" Dig into the threshold of His words and your tongue will speak life and blessing to yourself and the world.

The word of God becomes dead and powerless when your words start attacking His purposes for you. Every manufacturer has what he has in mind when manufacturing a particular product. It will be a tragedy for the product to turn around and attack the purpose for which it was designed. A drama in which the protagonist is overcome by some superior force or circumstance excites terror or pity. An event resulting in great loss and misfortune evokes tragedy. So think about the things you say about yourself. For instance; *"How can someone like me be visited with good things... please talk of something else. Have you not heard that in my family no one amounts to anything? Please, I am satisfied just knowing Jesus."* This is blind, boastful humility amounting to self-arrogated humiliation that God never assigns you and it gives Him no glory. To some extent, the Bible does teach that we rejoice in suffering if it is the will of God that we pass through such an event in our lives because, to some degree, it can help us to become and remain humble before God. There may be many things He wants to teach us in line with our union with Him. This does not suffice to say that we go about looking for suffering: *"Suffering where are you, please I want to be humble like Jesus."* NO! Think of this:

> *6 In this you greatly rejoice, though now for a little while, if need be, you have been grieved by various trials, 7 that the genuineness of your faith, being much more precious than gold that perishes, though it is tested by fire, may be found to praise, honor, and glory at the revelation of Jesus Christ. (1 Peter 1:6-7, NKJV)*

It is not what your parents, relatives, members, or friends always say about you that counts but what you believe and say about yourself. Your own perceptions, that is, how you become aware of something via the senses and the way you conceive of those things, can either build you up or bring you down. What you believe and say about yourself can also destroy your hope, change your case or keep you in a position, demote you, or bring lasting healing on you or sickness and disease. Once, on a mission with six other missionaries, I went to a certain African community that was trapped in very deadly wickedness and witchcraft practices. There were reports that they could poison soft drinks or other drinks with or without opening them. And they served us Coke and other soft drinks. One of the missionaries took the first sip and shouted out, *"Oh, I am dead. I did not remember that these people can poison drinks without opening them!"* On the spot, he dropped dead. The rest of us drank our own, including his drink, and are still alive today strongly proclaiming the good news to the nations. Beloved, what you say and believe can determine your fate. It was not magic or witchcraft that killed my associate but the terror he believed in his own mind, most likely causing a heart-failure. I am a living proof of this fact from many years in the jungles of Africa.

You are greatly influenced by your words, both you and the lives of those around you. You chart unawares the course of your life by the constant negative things you say. When God is moving forward, you are drawing Him backward and showing how nothing has ever worked where you are. Stop it right now and queue in to what the cross offers you. The word of God is the word of your faith. It is His factory by which He manufactures things. Someone once said:

> *God, you do not seem to understand my plight. In this town people who own degrees die at convocation hall – that is why am afraid of graduating. I wish there was someone who could enrol me in the next city college. God, wait, sit down and let us talk. My mother died in a car accident in the month of June. Abraham, my father, died in the same month along with Job, my elder brother. Moses, my first cousin and my sister, died in the same month as did my mother, Dorcas. My car almost killed me. Now I am feeling a headache because June is approaching. So God, this is what am saying, can you not understand? What are you saying or even thinking of me? Tell me – will I die or live?*

This is wickedness my friend. Stop accusing God of being a weakling who is incapable of handling your situation. Find out that in the same place you find yourself failing, others are making it. What makes you a great man or woman of God is the ability to see beyond what others can see, to see opportunity where others are failing:

> **Now faith is the substance of things hoped for, the evidence of things not seen. 2 For by it the elders obtained a good testimony. (Hebrews 11:1-2, NKJV)**

Your parents and others may have helped to put you on the road called *nothingness*; fine, but now say this, "*The Lord knows the way I take, He alone direct the steps of the righteous."* Refuse to walk on that negative ancestral road. Revolt against the system and break the crouches of its powers by the fire of God. Create a new, safer road that will lead to your destiny – the highway of glory, of perfection, of honour, of holiness, of power, of excellence. Courageously help place and position others on their destiny road. When you have won, help others to win. When you have reached the city, do not break the bridge so that other pilgrims can still pass there. Do not be an ingrate who locks the door against an honest seeker.

The life you are living, in part, is the picture of what you said and did in past days. Words are seeds of life. Today take your time to select the best of them. Make them soft, simple and delicious for some day, unawares, you will be made to eat them all. That you do not believe in the law of gravity and lift does not change its function nor stop it from keeping you on the ground or landing you down when you jump up. What goes up must come down. That you do not believe in the power of words does not elude it from working. Look at what the Bible has to say concerning God's own word:

> *For the word of God is living and powerful, and sharper than any two-edged sword, piercing even to the division of soul and spirit, and of joints and marrow, and is a*

discerner of the thoughts and intents of the heart.
(Hebrews 4:12, NKJV)

Your tongue can either give you life or death. It is, therefore, up to you to choose rightly or wrongly. You get what you choose. Practice saying what is right and good in God's eyes about yourself. Until you start seeing something good in you, you will not see it in another person. If you cannot appreciate yourself, you cannot appreciate another – even your spouse and children. If you do not like what you are doing, how then will you love what others are doing?

> *The Lord is my light and my salvation; Whom shall I fear? The Lord is the strength of my life; Of whom shall I be afraid? (Psalm 27:1, NKJV)*

> *That I would see the goodness of the Lord In the land of the living. (Psalm 27:13b, NKJV)*

> *The lines have fallen to me in pleasant places; Yes, I have a good inheritance. (Psalm 16:6, NKJV)*

> *1 The Lord is my shepherd; I shall not want ... 4 Yea, though I walk through the valley of the shadow of death [life vexing problems, trials], I will fear no evil; For You are with me; Your rod [discipline] and Your staff [guidance, leadership], they comfort me [embolden, sustain me]. (Psalm 23:1,4, NKJV)*

Keep saying these things without fear or doubt and be a life flowing river to yourself and others.

Help, Lord, for the godly man [the dependable man] ceases! For the faithful [the trusted, the reliable, and the man who can hold matters in strict confidence] disappear from among the sons of men. (Psalm 12:1, NKJV)

Oh Lord, where are you? Please make haste to help us! People you could trust with your matters or issues (your private details) and people with whom you could break the ice have ceased. Spouses, fathers, mothers, pastors and counsellors with whom you could show your tears, have failed. They use my dirty linens, my napkins, oh my private pampers as new commodities to display for gainful trade. They use it to form news headlines in the city news dailies. God's truth has gone to prison without a rescuer. Oh God, truth has lost it tongue. Ah! How I wish that truth could have a retainable tongue. These cacophonies speak empty, sweeping, enticing, palatable lies, vanities with bold faces, idle words that romance their hearers, selecting their words as cleverly as ornaments to attack their neighbours. Having their faces like executive angels visiting the White House, they grab innocent, ignorant souls with words without composited evidence. With lips that sound like an early morning feast and with a double-folder heart, they speak words that are sugar-coated to cheaply appeal to the palette of their listeners. Smiling majestically as when Jesus Of Good Hope visited the void toils of Peter by the sea side: *"That's alright, Peter Void Toiler, that is why I am here, to change the menu on your table, and the echo disparaged shoes you are wearing. You may not need to know how, but by the time I am done you will become the new Bishop of Oron Diocese and your eyes will be as swift as rockets."* At the end, guess what? Nothing happens.

> **2 They speak idly everyone with his neighbor; With flattering lips and a double heart they speak. 3 May the Lord cut off all flattering lips, And the tongue that speaks proud things, 4 Who have said, "With our tongue we will prevail; Our lips are our own; Who is lord over us?" (Psalm 12:2-4, NKJV)**

A day comes when the Lord of justice will cut off flattering lips and the tongue that speaks great swelling things without respect for God or human dignity. Those who have said, *"Our lips belong to us – we have no governor."* That is fine. But because of the affliction, devastation and groaning of the needy, *"Now I will arise..."* says the Lord of judgment, *"I will set him in the safety for which he yearns."* (Psalm 12:5, NKJV) The Lord has promised to bring deliverance to all who have been victims of dubious speakers, because His words are as pure and valuable as fully refined silver.

> **19 "I call heaven and earth as witnesses today against you, that I have set before you life and death, blessing and cursing; therefore choose life, that both you and your descendants may live; 20 that you may love the Lord your God, that you may obey His voice, and that you may cling to Him, for He is your life and the length of your days;**

THE POWER OF GOD'S WORD TO TRANSFORM YOUR LIFE

and that you may dwell in the land which the Lord swore to your fathers, to Abraham, Isaac, and Jacob, to give them." (Deuteronomy 30:19-20, NKJV)

Today, as long as you live on the earth, heaven and earth stand as great witnesses against you that life and death, curse and blessing are arranged before you as real destiny proposals. Whatever your choice, it will be justified for you and your posterity to live or die, cursed or blessed. The victory in the battle of life is for those who hold firm to the end. Your words should not quit you and your posterity. If you are a mother, father, mentor, or leader of people, what do you speak daily to those who are under your tutelage, to your subjects, children and dependents? If you do not quit, God will not quit. Never turn your situation into another prison.

And you, fathers, do not provoke your children to wrath, but bring them up in the training and admonition of the Lord. (Ephesians 6:4, NKJV)

21 Fathers, do not provoke your children, lest they become discouraged. 22 Bondservants, obey in all things your masters [don't grumble nor speak things above your intelligence] according to the flesh, not with eyeservice, as men-pleasers, but in sincerity of heart, fearing God. (Colossians 3:21-22, NKJV)

Mind what you say about your mother, father, pastors, rulers and others in authority over you. If not, it can destroy your future, sending it into curses that may multiply and even impact the next generation. This is one of the reasons for repeated tragic history in families, and nations. Most often we say damaging words as a result of indefinable fear and insecurity. You start talking and behaving as a wild animal in a cafe seeking escape. Instead, learn to be on your best behaviour – no matter what – so that God can answer on your behalf and be a miracle to you.

One major problem about fear is that it can divert you from your destiny. Fear breeds fears – that is why it is called in Bible psychology "dragon" *(drag-on)*. There is no animal you will see in the bush or forest or the water anywhere called *dragon*. It is the fear of the unknown. It may be phobia or anti-phobia. When it captures you as a P.O.W (prisoner of war), it will drag you down, on and on, unless you grab the hands of Christ for help. Hang your case on God's unchangeable hands for He will not fail you.

> *14 Inasmuch then as the children have partaken of flesh and blood, He Himself likewise shared in the same, that through death He might destroy him who had the power of death, that is, the devil, 15 and release those who through fear of death were all their lifetime subject to bondage. 16 For indeed He does not give aid to angels, but He does give aid to the seed of Abraham. 17 Therefore, in all things He had to be made like His brethren, that He might be a merciful and faithful High Priest in things pertaining to God, to make propitiation for the sins of the people. 18 For in that He Himself has*

suffered, being tempted, He is able to aid those who are tempted. (Hebrews 2:14-18, NKJV)

On the other hand, boldness speaks courage, words of faith:

1 Now faith is the substance of things hoped for, the evidence of things not seen. 2 For by it the elders obtained a good testimony. 3 By faith we understand that the worlds were framed by the word of God, so that the things which are seen were not made of things which are visible. 4 By faith Abel offered to God a more excellent sacrifice than Cain, through which he obtained witness that he was righteous, God testifying of his gifts; and through it he being dead still speaks. 5 By faith Enoch was taken away so that he did not see death, "and was not found, because God had taken him"; for before he was taken he had this testimony, that he pleased God. 6 But without faith it is impossible to please Him, for he who comes to God must believe that He is, and that He is a rewarder of those who diligently seek Him. (Hebrews 11:1-5, NKJV)

The story of King David fleeing from Absalom, his own son, tells the tragic results of fear over faith:

10 Then Absalom sent spies throughout all the tribes of Israel, saying, "As soon as you hear the sound of the trumpet, then you shall say, 'Absalom reigns in Hebron!'" 11 And with Absalom went two hundred men invited from Jerusalem, and they went along innocently and did not know anything. 12 Then Absalom sent for Ahithophel the Gilonite, David's counselor, from his city—from Giloh—while he offered sacrifices. And the conspiracy grew strong, for the people with Absalom continually increased in number. 13 Now a messenger came to David, saying, "The hearts of the men of Israel are with Absalom." 14 So David said to all his servants who were with him at Jerusalem, "Arise, and let us flee, or we shall not escape from Absalom. Make haste to depart, lest he overtake us suddenly and bring disaster upon us, and strike the city with the edge of the sword." 15 And the king's servants said to the king, "We are your servants, ready to do whatever my lord the king commands." 16 Then the king went out with all his household after him. But the king left ten women, concubines, to keep the house. 17 And the king went out with all the people after him, and stopped at the outskirts. 18 Then all his servants passed before him; and all the Cherethites, all the Pelethites, and all the Gittites, six hundred men who had followed him from Gath, passed before the king. 19 Then the king said to Ittai the Gittite, "Why are you also going with us? Return and remain with the king. For you are a foreigner and also an exile from your own place. 20 In fact, you came only yesterday. Should I make you wander up and down with us today, since I go I know not where? Return, and take your brethren back. Mercy and truth be with you." 21 But Ittai answered the king and said, "As the Lord lives, and as my lord the king lives, surely in whatever place my lord the king shall be, whether in death or life, even there also your servant will be." (2 Samuel 15:10-21, NKJV)

What a sad story that a son, subjects, and relatives could displace their father, pastor, leader and friend. My good friend and family member of the household of faith, how do you feel inside as you read this account? I feel like lying down, prostrated and crying bitterly for the many Christ kings that have run to the bush because of fear of their sons, daughters, family members, and subordinates. It now defines their line of actions and command to all under them. Fear has taken nations down into endless conflicts, wars, sagas, mayhems that have wet the hard soil of their land with the hot blood of precious souls who never saw their dreams. *"Arise let us flee for we shall not escape ..."* (2 Samuel 15:14, NKJV) In the name above every other name, even Yashua Hamashua, any power or evil personality that is pursuing you:

- Out of office to the bush of despair
- Out of your marriage
- Out of your sweet, out of your ministry
- Out of your dreams to catch fire and die

In the earthshaking name of Jesus Christ, may they be confounded that seek your down fall in the name of Jesus. What pursues you, pursue it now in the mighty name of Jesus Christ. In 2 Samuel 15:14, NKJV they reported fear, panic and defeat to a whole, divinely anointed warhorse: Jehovah`s General Army Commander – a Priest and king of a royal priesthood; a leader of peculiar people; an Apostle of a chosen generation; a Bishop of a nation and assembly of Jehovah El-Shaddai. Oh, a prophet of the Most High, a Judge with Yahweh`s special choice, unquenchable supernatural king and priest, dismantling anointing of a kind through fear from malicious and acrimonious report of cynics rose up and fled. Ah! Hear him saying *"Arise, let us flee, there is no more hope for our escape, here is the end, there is a surprise*

attack, evil is about to come upon us, the city will die by sword"
Instead your words should be:

"Ah! God, my Jehovah Nisi, my Ebenezer, my hope in the time of war, and my Shiloh, arise! Arise and respond firmly, positively and decisively to every ancient dragon dragging on and on your heroes of war, your veterans, your army, and your very seed for whom you died. Like a mighty wind, sweep them off and confront my confronters that have arisen from within my own loins, my ranks, my household to challenge me out of my palace of glory and honour, rewarding evil for all my good. Lord, let them see the fire in Your eyes so that they will flee like rams into their destruction in the earthshaking name of Jesus Christ of Nazareth, the very Son of the Most High God, the great I AM THAT I AM."

Amen! Confess the following scriptures of abundance at the top of your voice:

1. I delight myself in the word of the Lord, therefore, I am blessed. Wealth and riches shall be in my house and my righteousness endures forever. (Psalm 112:1-3)
2. God is able to make all grace abound toward me, which I will always have all sufficiency in all things and may have an abundance for every good work. (2 Corinthians 9:8)
3. I remember the Lord my God, for it is He that gives me power to get wealth. (Deuteronomy 8:18)
4. I am crowned with wealth. (Proverbs 14:24)

5. With me are riches and honour, enduring wealth and prosperity. (Proverbs 8:18)

After making the confessions above, begin to pray like this… with a loud voice:

1. O God arise and let my head be lifted up in Jesus' name.
2. O Lord, release unto me your angels of prosperity in the name of Jesus (shout this 21 times).
3. Every mouth anointed to curse my blessings, O LORD, transfer their arrows back to them in the mighty name of Jesus.
4. Any curse of poverty transmitted through my bloodlines, break, break, break, in the name of Jesus.
5. Satanic chains and padlocks locking my blessings, break, break, break in the mighty name of Jesus.
6. Any altar where my blessings are shared in the spirit, catch fire and burn to ashes in the name of Jesus.

Amen!

---

[1] Source unknown.

From Victim to Victor

Chapter Six
Choices and Your Tomorrow

4 Look also at ships: although they are so large and are driven by fierce winds, they are turned by a very small rudder wherever the pilot desires. 5 Even so the tongue is a little member and boasts great things. See how great a forest a little fire kindles! 6 And the tongue is a fire, a world of iniquity. The tongue is so set among our members that it defiles the whole body, and sets on fire the course of nature; and it is set on fire by hell. 7 For every kind of beast and bird, of reptile and creature of the sea, is tamed and has been tamed by mankind. 8 But no man can tame the tongue. It is an unruly evil, full of deadly poison. 9 With it we bless our God and Father, and with it we curse men, who have been made in the similitude of God. 10 Out of the same mouth proceed blessing and cursing. My brethren, these things ought not to be so. 11 Does a spring send forth fresh water and bitter from the same opening? (James 3:4-11, NKJV)

This passage of Scripture highlights what the tongue is and what it can do – negatively and positively. The understanding gained here will filter slowly into what we will be discussing throughout this chapter. I pray that the Holy Spirit will guide you to best understand what this chapter is intended to teach you. It will change you and make you experience the mind of Christ for you.

Many good and loving people suffer, perhaps including yourself. We do not know why but God knows. The are many more questions than answers. But He alone understands. He has not called us to explanations but promises. When you stand on the way of promise as He is moving and visiting, He will fulfill His promises concerning you. May He so find you standing by what you say and believe.

Back in 2001, I was preaching in a church when the host pastor asked me to pray for a young man who had a problem for many years. The young man said, *"Man of God, no, because I know God can do anything but not in my case. He cannot do anything to help me. I have been in this situation for six years."* It is not an easy way we are traveling to Heaven but He makes us willing to go. In His word He gives us sufficient weapons which, if we can select them with good comprehension, we can secure today and tomorrow. When the storms rage and darkness hides the stars, His voice makes the difference.

From my experience as a missionary who lived and ran a selfless life and ministry, becoming a libation poured daily on the rock of eternal sacrifice and a foot carpet for many to step into the kingdom of God, I can testify that His voice makes the difference. When He speaks, He relieves my troubled mind. It gives me direction and guides my mouth in what to say in any situation. It has helped me to follow Him, one day at a time, for the journey of a million miles begins with just one step. It has calmed many storms and torn down many strongholds in my life. It has turned my darkness around. As a sheep knows the voice of the master, so have I always known His voice and learned to say those things He wants me to say, things that rather embarrass and cause havoc to the devil and his workers.

Bad things happen to good and genuine people. They go through life with so much pain and hardship to the point of believing that perhaps this is the will of God for them, so as to be humble and holy. They even believe that it is the way of life allotted to them by God so that they could be sanctified enough for heaven. Some conclude that while bad and wicked people live happily, the saints should be singing and weeping passionately. So we have such songs as:

- "You may take the whole world, all cars, house, good wives and husbands, promotion, I belong to Jesus, and I am satisfied."
- "Today, today, tomorrow no more, if I die today, I will die no more."
- "On earth, I weep, in Heaven I shall smile in the streets of gold."

But I challenge you that if there shall be any Heaven, then your dancing and singing should begin here right now. I should start here to sing my song and dance my dance. The question one would need ask himself is this: how scripturally inspired are these songs for us today who are in Christ Jesus? Jesus has paid the price for us at Calvary. The cross has settled it all. As far as our faith in the finished work of Christ on the cross is concerned, beloved, believe it or not, there are some Scriptures that do not directly apply to believers today. For instance, to apply Old Covenant rules to New Covenant Christianity is not correct. Find out in the Bible what really applies to your particular case that is compatible with what Christ has done for you on the cross. The devil hears these self-consoling, lamentation songs and laughs to scorn. Why? Because he knows that you are ignorant of what Christ has done for you. These kinds of songs also reveal your belief system. I encourage you to change the music and your confession to match the word of God for your life. Do not be upset with your case. Let it not overwhelm you, dragging you away from the truth of God's will for you.

Allow me to embarrass your reasoning a little bit to bring you to hidden truths you need to know to stay connected to the source of your faith and hold unto God's unchanging hands that will never grow too weak to carry you. Life has never promised an easy passage to anyone. Nor has the Saviour ever said that it will be all rosy as we come into relationship with Him. I know what some of you are going through right now. I have been there many times as I follow Him daily attempting to obey Him the best that I can through His grace. There have been many moments of darkness and desperation when I felt like quitting. But in such rivers and storms I receive the revelation of what I communicate to other lonely travelers. Desperation brings revelation. God gives us revelation to help our brothers and sisters in their perils so that they will not quit. The Bible is a complete revelation for our salvation.

Let us carefully examine what the Bible is communicating to us in John's gospel:

> *30 And truly Jesus did many other signs in the presence of His disciples, which are not written in this book; 31 but these are written that you may believe that Jesus is the Christ, the Son of God, and that believing you may have life in His name. (John 20:30-31, NKJV)*

Permit me to say that one of the most unique purposes of the Bible is to give us everything we need to know from the Lord to be saved or born again. Yet the Bible does not cover specific instructions for every single experience, fate and encounter in of your life; if it did, the Bible would require many trucks to carry all the volumes. But as we trust Him in our darkness through His word and prayers, He gives us revelations (*helping us understand His revealted truth in the Bible and how to apply it in our unique situation*) that produce actions that lead to the solution we need.

God's revelation will never end and never cease; it will continue to stream in for those who ask for it for God Himself is a God of revelation according to your need:

> *77 To give knowledge of salvation to His people By the remission of their sins, 78 Through the tender mercy of our God, With which the Dayspring from on high has visited us; 79 To give light to those who sit in darkness and the shadow of death, To guide our feet into the way of peace." (Luke1:77-79, NKJV)*

> *68 "Blessed is the Lord God of Israel, For He has visited and redeemed His people, 69 And has raised up a horn of salvation for us In the house of His servant David, 70 As He spoke by the mouth of His holy prophets, Who have been since the world began, 71 That we should be saved from our enemies And from the hand of all who hate us, 72 To perform the mercy promised to our fathers And to remember His holy covenant. (Luke 1:68-72, NKJV)*

Put your attention here and I pray that the Lord will open your eyes to understand the points I am trying to make:

- *He has visited [*come*] and redeemed [*delivered*] His people [*He has come and brought deliverance and redemption (soul salvation; His greatest gift to the unredeemed) to His people (first Israel then the Gentile believers*] (Luke 1:68, NKJV with author's amplification). Note the phrase *"His people"* the unbelievers are not His people until they have placed faith in Jesus as personal Lord and Saviour.
- *And has raised [*designed, pronounced, caused to be known, put forward for consideration, summoned into

action, called forth] *up a Horn* [not a device but speaking of strength, power and authority, battle force ready for any given situation] *of salvation* [setting free from the penalty, grip and total control of sin; daily deliverances; satisfaction in life; abundant life/living] *for us.* (Luke 1:69, NKJV with author's amplification)

- *To give* [deliver in exchange or recompense; cause to have; convey to; transfer the possession of; present to view; communicate] *knowledge* [the psychological result of perception, learning, and reasoning] *of salvation to His people.* (Luke 1:77, NKJV with author's amplification)

- *Through the tender* [Having or displaying warmth or affection.] *mercy* [mercy means exempt from judgment; leniency and compassion shown toward offenders by a person or agency charged with administering justice; alleviation of distress; showing great kindness toward the distressed; a disposition to be kind and forgiving] *of our God...* (Luke 1:78, NKJV with author's amplification)

- *That we should be saved from our enemies And from the hand of all who hate us.* (Luke 1:71, NKJV) Christ has not come to save us from the shackles of sin and then hand us over to the enemy and those who hate us to deal with us as they think we so deserve. He has not come to give us living water and then surrender us to the devil to parade about as if he cannot be molested so that he develops the audacity to feed us with bitter water, bread of sorrows and ashes mixed up as milk.

By the revelation of God's truth, I challenge you that no matter how many troubles may come – much as if need be you may sit in darkness, much as sometimes you may be under the shades of death – yet discover that most of your struggles,

FROM VICTIM TO VICTOR

sufferings and heavy burdens are quite unnecessary as far as God is concerned. The truth is that God does not need it to make you fit for rapture. It is not enough, for that would be too weak a method. The song writer says, *"lest I forget Gethsemane, Lord Take me back to Calvary ... Oh Calvary, Calvary, I would not forget Calvary."* What you need to do is to believe that – whatever you are going through – Jesus has been there before you. As the song continues, *"I need no augment, I need no other plea, it is enough that Jesus died and that He died for me."* As you experience want and lack, bankruptcy and penury, have your body ravaged with all kind of indefinable sickness; your home vandalise, name it all, understand that the suffering itself does not give God glory for one minute. What glorifies God in your time of suffering is seeing you faithfully trust in Jesus and what He suffered for you.

I am asking the Holy Spirit to help you understand this crucial attitude. Yes, you will have tribulations in the world; but be of good spirit for Jesus has overcome the world. I do not live in the defeat of my despair but in the victory of the cross. Jesus conquered death, sin, and the devil's plan. I should believe it, speak it and challenge every rage of the devil against my destiny with the revelation this fact gives me. Lord, thank You for this condition, but I am glad that over 2,000 years ago, before I was born, before this problem cropped up, You overcame sin and the devil's plan, giving me the victory. Therefore, by the power of

Your death on the cross, I have victory now over every power assigned to trouble me. Devil, hear the word of the Lord: I am an Overcomer, I am a conqueror, you can do me no harm for Jesus overcome you on the cross. Therefore, be silent and move out of my way in the name of Jesus Christ.

Sometimes, for our pride, Jesus will put you in the ring for the devil to punch it out. Then He will show up neatly and tangibly. He may delay if we are complaining, fidgeting and crying until we call on Him to be delivered. Greater is He that is in you than he that is out there in the world (1 John 4:4). Get the revelation of what He has be done and turn it into your confession – live a life worthy of His calling (Ephesians 4:1):

14 Inasmuch then as the children have partaken of flesh and blood, He Himself likewise shared in the same, that through death He might destroy him who had the power of death, that is, the devil, 15 and release those who through fear of death were all their lifetime subject to bondage. 16 For indeed He does not give aid to angels, but He does give aid to the seed of Abraham. 17 Therefore, in all things He had to be made like His brethren, that He might be a merciful and faithful High Priest in things pertaining to God, to make propitiation for the sins of the people. 18 For in that He Himself has suffered, being tempted, He is able to aid those who are tempted. (Hebrews 2:14-18, NKJV)

2 Beloved, I pray that you may prosper in all things and be in health, just as your soul prospers. 3 For I rejoiced greatly when brethren came and testified of the truth that is in you, just as you walk in the truth. 4 I have no greater joy than to hear that my children walk in truth. 5 Beloved, you do faithfully whatever you do for the brethren and for strangers ... 11 Beloved, do not imitate what is evil, but what is good. He who does good is of God, but he who does evil has not seen God. 12 Demetrius has a good testimony from all, and from the truth itself. And we also bear witness, and you know that our testimony is true. (3 John 2-5,11-12, NKJV)

As a missionary, I know what I have gone through in my obedience to obey God with my life in an attempt to carry the message of the cross to many dark corners of the earth. Sometimes my tea has been poisoned by Bishops. I have escaped many physical deaths by pastors and wickedness of the highest order. To some extent, it conforms to what is written:

9 but they will progress no further, for their folly will be manifest to all, as theirs also was. 10 But you have carefully followed my doctrine, manner of life, purpose, faith, longsuffering, love, perseverance, 11 persecutions, afflictions, which happened to me at Antioch, at Iconium, at Lystra—what persecutions I endured. And out of them all the Lord delivered me. 12 Yes, and all who desire to live godly in Christ Jesus will suffer persecution. 13 But evil men and impostors will grow worse and worse, deceiving and being deceived. 14 But you must continue in the things which you have learned and been assured of, knowing from whom you have learned them. (2 Timothy 3:9-14)

By His grace in 1978 August 14th the Lord spoke to me in an unmistakeable manner that I cannot forget: "Son, teach and preach the 'front and back of the cross.' Take my cup, my heart, my love and forgiveness to my people all over the world." Before this time, I had a horrible accident that passersby and eye witnesses could never believe that I would make it or survive it. I was riding on auto-bike that was completely destroyed. I was going to minister in a Scripture Union revival meeting some 60 miles from my station. A heavy ITC truck hit me and ran away. My shoes, helmet and wrist watch were found several yards away. Everything scattered and I was by the road side. The first thing my hands could grab was a small tree – but with the force of the collision I pulled up the tree. At that point, people rushed in and held me, blood flowing and gushing out of every part of me. When I opened my mouth, blood issued like a flood. That fateful moment, I shouted out loud, "Jesus of Nazareth, in this situation prove to the world and these people standing here the very purpose of your death on the cross. Did you die so that I should also die prematurely as you did? If not, then I, Covenant David Livingstone, will not die but live. I have not yet begun – I am just getting started!" then I turn to the devil and said, "You, Satan, hell and grave, my father's house, my ancestors and you that hate my destiny – Jesus on the cross died prematurely for me that I should not die shamefully before my glory is revealed to the world. I am a child and servant of God. You cannot kill me."

I focused on the cross and the purpose of why Christ came. The only medication I took was Vaseline for rubbing the wounds and the Lord's supper. Today, to Him alone be the glory, I am alive and you shall live and not die. Any power that wants to kill you before your glory is revealed, die in the name of Jesus Christ. Evil personalities that want to see your obituary, let them die in your place in the mighty name of Jesus Christ. The front of the cross has to do with our redemption from sin and Satan. The back of the cross speaks of the revelation of what the cross can do for us in our time here on Earth.

God has no physical body - the Bible says He is "**Spirit**" (John 4:24, NKJV). When He told Moses, "**you shall see My back; but My face shall not be seen**" (Exodus 33:23, NKJV), it was not like yours and mine. All God could reveal to Moses without killing him was His receding glory. But His revelation changed Moses. After being "**with the Lord forty days and forty nights**" (Exodus 34:28, NKJV), Moses received the revelations for the book of Genesis and events that took place in the dateless past before Moses was born. God's people are destroyed, not for lack of knowledge of my word since every man can fathom something out of it. But, "**Where there is no revelation, the people cast off** restraint; **But happy is he who keeps the law.**" (Proverbs 29:18, NKJV). The times and days of preaching, teaching and dwelling on the surface-level of the Bible has faded away. May God give you the revelation of His word today and His joy as you obey it.

All you need is the cross where you enter into His plan for your life and identify with that purpose. Christ is the wisdom of God and wisdom is power and victory. Sometimes God reveals things to you before they happen to show you that He does not want it to happen. When you do not pray and sometimes call for friends and the church to help in prayer, it may not happen. The authorities killed James and the people rejoiced. Since that sounded like a good thing, they move forward to kill Peter (Acts 12:1-4). **"But constant prayer was offered to God for him by the church"** (Acts 12:5, NKJV) and God sent an Angel to deliver Peter. Everyone in the fellowship had a piece of Dorcas but she fell sick and died without even the pastor neither knowing nor praying for her case or illness. Thank God that Peter came and Dorcas came back to life. Every member of church, including the pastors, passed a beggar and gave him help to remain a beggar until Peter and his team arrived. Peter offered the beggar the wisdom and power of God; his begging syndrome become a past tense. Prayerfully examine what Jesus said: "And you shall know the truth, and the truth shall make you free." (John 8:32, NKJV).

Rightly put, "you shall know the truth, but the truth that you personally know and accept is the truth that sets you free."

Let me say here that what I am helping you to see in this chapter (even the entire book) has nothing to do with suffering and the believer's position or attitude in accordance with the revealed truth in God's word. That I will talk about in my next book, coming soon, entitled "The Unclaimed Promise." The concentration here is for you to see the importance of God's word becoming your words.

> 23 "For there is no sorcery against Jacob, Nor any divination [the pretence of prophecy by demonic means] against Israel. It now must be said of Jacob And of Israel, 'Oh, what God has done!' 24 Look, a people rises like a lioness, And lifts itself up like a lion; It shall not lie down until it devours the prey, And drinks the blood of the slain." (Numbers 23:23-24, NKJV)

This, I believe, applies to me today as it did for Israel thousands of years ago. For the Lord to say something like this, it certainly means that there are enchanters and enchantment; there abound diviners and divination in every nation. Even if you do not believe it, yet it is true. That you don't believe in the devil and demons do not mean he does not exist. You are just like an atheist who says not only in his heart but in his behaviours that there is no God. Does that mean to say that God does not exist? Your words cannot win when they go against God and His word. You must believe and agree to and speak out what is in agreement with God. That is your key to success.

> *15 Indeed they shall surely assemble, but not because of Me. Whoever assembles against you shall fall for your sake. 16 "Behold, I have created the blacksmith Who blows the coals in the fire, Who brings forth an instrument for his work; And I have created the spoiler to destroy. 17 No weapon formed against you shall prosper, And every tongue which rises against you in judgment You shall condemn. This is the heritage of the servants of the Lord, And their righteousness is from Me," Says the Lord. (Isaiah 54:15-17, NKJV)*

Two key points need to be considered in this passage that was directed to Israel but has application to believers in Christ. Verse 15 indicates *"they shall surely assemble"* but God has not instructed them to assemble showing that there is an evil purpose to the assemblies against innocent souls and the rigidly righteous. Then if God cannot instruct or command such a gathering, what should I do – thank them and cook food for them or lie down and wait for them to do what they want? Second, verse 17 says that *"no weapon fashioned against you shall prosper"* – again, indicating that there would be some persons fashioning weapons to destroy you. It may be the weapon of the tongue. Oh, every tongue that shall rise against the LORD in judgment shall be condemned. This is the heritage of the servants of the LORD, and

123

their righteousness. Every tongue that says evil against you will be judged false. *"This is the heritage of the servants of the Lord, and their righteousness is from Me,' says the Lord."* *(Isaiah 54:17, NKJV)*

Who will condemn it – is it the Lord, the Holy Spirit, the pastor or some powerful Justice? It says "YOU" will condemn it or prove it to be false. The day you start allowing the word of God to come alive in your believing and value system is the day your mouth will say things that will change your life and those around you. There abound people that if you go to them with only an ounce of faith, you will return wretched and empty because of what they speak out. Words are light, spirit and life. If you speak defeat, and curses and all kind of filth and negative words, it promotes death. If you speak the word of God and positive encouraging words, it promotes life.

The devil knows how powerful and impactful words can be so he uses them as a weapon. But we encounter him and his evil men around us with anointed words built upon the word of God and the cross. Philosophy will not be successful as I found with one of my pastor friends. Back in 1979 a certain woman had provoked him and he challenged her as a philosopher. Only later did he remember that he was a Christian so he spoke some

Christian words with her. I told my friend, *"You have failed and shamed God."*

22 that you put off, concerning your former conduct, the old man which grows corrupt according to the deceitful lusts, 23 and be renewed in the spirit of your mind, 24 and that you put on the new man which was created according to God, in true righteousness and holiness. 25 Therefore, putting away lying, "Let each one of you speak truth with his neighbor,"[a] for we are members of one another. (Ephesians 4:22-25, NKJV)

Do not curse the king, even in your thought; Do not curse the rich, even in your bedroom; For a bird of the air may carry your voice, And a bird in flight may tell the matter.Do not revile the king even in your thoughts, or curse the rich in your bedroom, because a bird in the sky may carry your words, and a bird on the wing may report what you say. (Ecclesiastes 10:20, NKJV)

36 But I say to you that for every idle word men may speak, they will give account of it in the day of judgment. 37 For by your words you will be justified, and by your words you will be condemned. (Matthew 12:36-37, NKJV)

11 And their words seemed to them like idle tales, and they did not believe them. 12 But Peter arose and ran to the tomb; and stooping down, he saw the linen cloths lying by themselves; and he departed, marveling to himself at what had happened. (Luke 24:11-12, NKJV)

And besides they learn to be idle, wandering about from house to house, and not only idle but also gossips and

busybodies, saying things which they ought not.
(1Timothy 5:13, NKJV)

How many people have entered into untold troubles by what they say!

- Some have been killed
- Some sent to prison
- Some cause the death of others
- Some lose their jobs for another
- Some lose their marriage
- Some create lasting enmity, conflicts and wars

I challenge you today – please do not destroy tomorrow by what you say today. Some children today all over the world are suffering the consequences of problems their parents created with their mouth and lifestyle. Consider and read meditatively: *"7 Our fathers sinned and are no more, But we bear their iniquities. 8 Servants rule over us; There is none to deliver us from their hand. (Lamentations 5:7-8, NKJV)*Nations suffer and go through endless, meaningless wars because of what their political leaders say. Most world leaders who came in with palatable promises end up creating more problems for their people without solving existing ones on the ground. That is why we have of recent witness the Arab spring, the Occupied Wall Street in New York and the seizing of an Anglican Church in London. Over the ages, words have created untold injuries, havoc, damage, and financial wastage. Insensitive foul languages will one day feed you with bitter regrets. Avoid it now and be sensitive – ask God to help you rightly use your tongue.

Start studying God's word and meditate on it. Speak it as your words until it saturates your whole life. Remove your eyes from how dark and gloomy it is now, for you know not what God is planning for you. He has a future for believers that no man has seen nor has it been told to any man. Even if it so pleases God to permit certain unexpected events to take place, yet honour Him with your words. Most great hymns come from the lips of men who were visited with the unexpected. I was in a certain missionary area when war broke out between three antagonistic communities. Churches were burned and pastors, along with members and their families, were beheaded. My school prefect (or head of students) was beheaded with his wife. A government journalist who came to cover our convocation was burned beyond recognition. My library worth over $30,000 was burned. My two Forerunners (a Sport Utility Vehicle) and two Hovercrafts were seized and destroyed. My account of $5,000 was burned in the bank that was looted. The only thing I came out with was my reading glass and the Bible I always love holding. In the area where I lived, I was the only missionary who survived. That experience has placed my hands into my laps today. People were watching to hear what I would say or cry out to Satan. The Lord has taught me not to allow the devil to see my tears. The only thing that came out of my mouth was a song that has remained as an instrument for building my faith (*"I made up my mind to serve the Lord"* was the song).

> *19 Remember my affliction and roaming, The wormwood and the gall. 20 My soul still remembers And sinks within me. 21 This I recall to my mind, Therefore I have hope. 22 Through the Lord's mercies we are not consumed, Because His compassions fail not. 23 They are new every morning; Great is Your faithfulness. 24 "The Lord is my portion," says my soul, "Therefore I hope in Him!" 25 The Lord is good to those who wait for Him, To the soul who seeks Him. 26 It is good that one should hope and wait quietly For the salvation of the Lord. (Lamentations 3:19-26, NKJV)*

See how your life is like a ship with the goods of life for the world about to be delivered to where it is needed most. It has been positioned by God and His word in the waters of life for sails but He made you the captain. As the captain, you have a civic responsibility to direct the ship with the impulse of the choice of your words, lubricate it with much patience, grease it with the right attitude and understanding, and balance the sails with humility built by the simplicity of the gospel and trusting obedience. A young man had gone through the University graduate with a Masters in Banking and Finance. One day his pastor's friend asked the pastor to bring him to begin working in one of the reputable Banks. He told the pastor, *"Pastor, I am tired today –*

tomorrow please take me there." So the pastor told his friend what the young man had said. The pastor's friend determined that the young man was not serious. It is about seven years now and the young man has no steady job – he is now polishing shoes by the road side just to avert being a nuisance. It is up to you, not God, to start using your tongue to benefit yourself today and for tomorrow.

> **8 This Book of the Law shall not depart from your mouth, but you shall meditate in it day and night, that you may observe to do according to all that is written in it. For then you will make your way prosperous, and then you will have good success. 9 Have I not commanded you? Be strong and of good courage; do not be afraid, nor be dismayed, for the Lord your God is with you wherever you go. (Joshua 1:8-9, NKJV)**

Many circumstances may confuse and confound you:

1. When the devil starts messing up things in your life
2. Your life calling may be attracting trouble
3. You might not be standing in front of the rightful door for your destiny (God wants you to change direction)
4. Your ministry or service may be finished and you are needed somewhere else
5. The time to be there may not be ripe
6. There is something in you to be contested
7. When men rough-handle you (unwittingly they are preparing you for greater height and glory and arranging themselves for judgment and demotion)

8. You have overstayed your welcome
9. God may be bragging about you before Satan (remember what happened to Job)

Never panic but watch what comes out of your mouth. God may be testing you to prove the genuineness of your faith:

- To find character in you
- To find Himself in you
- To see what you will do – whether you will give glory to Him or the devil
- To refine you and to make you His polished shaft and your tongue like the pen of a ready writer

Do not say what the devil wants to hear, and never let him see your tears. Rather, say what God wants to hear. In every temptation there is a way of escape. If it comes not or delays yet, God will always come at the right time. He is the God of the eleventh hour. Join David in saying:

> *The Lord is my shepherd; I shall not want. 2 He makes me to lie down [relax, calm] in green pastures [His providence]; He leads me beside the still waters [place of God's favor]. 3 He restores [revives, heals, and lifts up] my soul; He leads [directs, guards, guides] me in the paths of righteousness For His name's sake. 4 Yea, though I walk through the valley of the shadow of death [frightful, turbulent, life-demanding condition], I will fear no evil; For You are with me; Your rod [discipline, corrections] and Your staff [guidance, shepherding], they comfort me. 5 You prepare a table before me in the*

presence of my enemies; You anoint my head with oil; My cup runs over. 6 Surely goodness and mercy shall follow me All the days of my life; And I will dwell[a] in the house of the Lord Forever. (Psalm 23, NKJV)

FROM VICTIM TO VICTOR

Chapter Seven

Choices and the Word of God

So then faith comes by hearing, and hearing by the word of God. (Romans 10:17, NKJV)

2 This only I want to learn from you: Did you receive the Spirit by the works of the law, or by the hearing of faith? ... 5 Therefore He who supplies the Spirit to you and works miracles among you, does He do it by the works of the law, or by the hearing of faith? (Galatians 3:2,5, NKJV)

Let the word of Christ dwell in you richly in all wisdom, teaching and admonishing one another in psalms and hymns and spiritual songs, singing with grace in your hearts to the Lord. (Colossians 3:16, NKJV)

There are songs and hymns that build confession and faith. To speak devil-promoting words and negate the necessity of the word of God is to act as if you are bewitched. Tradition is the enemy of revelation. Drop your customs and tradition and what is familiar to you – that which your fathers have been speaking – and go by what the word of God has said. Yes, your condition is appalling, but be courageous. Sometimes people will not encourage but, instead, will debate the modality of your condition.

Look up and say what will glorify God. Miracles are not blown from the nose like mucous but cultivated by God in the life of believers who feed their faith with His word, eliminating doubts and fears. Starve your doubts and feed your faith like these believers of long ago:

16 Shadrach, Meshach, and Abed-Nego answered and said to the king, "O Nebuchadnezzar, we have no need to answer you in this matter. 17 If that is the case, our God whom we serve is able to deliver us from the burning fiery furnace, and He will deliver us from your hand, O king. 18 But if not, let it be known to you, O king, that we do not serve your gods, nor will we worship the gold image which you have set up." 19 Then Nebuchadnezzar was full of fury, and the expression on his face changed toward Shadrach, Meshach, and Abed-Nego. He spoke and commanded that they heat the furnace seven times more than it was usually heated. 20 And he commanded certain mighty men of valor who were in his army to bind Shadrach, Meshach, and Abed-Nego, and cast them into the burning fiery furnace. 21 Then these men were bound in their coats, their trousers, their turbans, and their other garments, and were cast into the midst of the burning fiery furnace. (Daniel 3:16-21, NKJV)

God recognized their steadfast faith and delivered them from the fire. And so the LORD presented a mighty sign to King Nebuchadnezzar and his court. Read the remaining account and see the outcome of their faith. What people think is your end by their own hand may just be the beginning with God. In Daniel 3:22-30 we see their vindication was by faith revealed in their spoken words in the midst of terror by the king of terror. Even King Nebuchadnezzar offered praise: *"Blessed be the God of Shadrach, Meshach, and Abed-Nego, who sent His Angel and delivered His servants who trusted in Him." (Daniel 3:28, NKJV)*

These Hebrew brethren made no bargain with God. They knew that with God both deliverance and martyrdom were possible. Yet Nebaba saw a greater one than Nebuchadnezzar: "CHRIST THE KING OF FIRE FURNACE" in his fire and bow. In every fire there is a second, third and fourth person. Fear not and speak to the devil that you are not his candidate and shall never be. These brethren never bowed and never burned. You, likewise, will not bow and will not burn out. The flames will reveal the gold and silver in you for the world to see. Only maintain your peace.

Their faith and words brought great glory and honour to God, the reward of lasting beauty to them, and even a promotion. Your faith-spoken words today are just as effective. Yes, *"Our God is able, My God, Your God, He is able, abundantly able to deliver those who trust in him."* Do not allow the jealous insinuations of the devil by his agents to frighten you or compromise your convictions. Instead, give a bold unhesitating witness to your allegiance to our ONE and only TRUE KING. In the midst of all that you may be going through now, develop a hope and a faith that is fixed on Jesus Christ – your refuge and your strength. Understand that the wrath of God against sin and disobedience is far worse than the wrath of men and the devil against you. Strive to be totally free from sin and Satan.

These three Hebrew brethren, in an expression of unconditional faith, complete trust and total loyalty to God, said, *"But if not..." (Daniel 3:18, NKJV)* You need to reach a level where you possess a faith, trust and obedience to God regardless of the consequences. Obedience and persevering trust in God and not necessarily the experience of deliverance, gives true evidence of Biblical faith. There are times that your faith may be tested. Keep in mind this is not for hatred or a sign to prove that God has abandoned you.

So then faith comes by hearing and by hearing by the word of God (Romans 10:17) preached about Christ and His finished work on the cross of Calvary. Hear those powerful messages from the godly lips of God's messengers, the pastors, prophets and so on – stand on them to build your confession and faith.

Chapter Eight
Choosing the August Release

Are you aware that every year, by the end of August, we come to the end of the second quarter of the year – the season of release? That is why, at this moment, it is important that I should lead you into some vital truths that you will need to achieve victory throughout your life.

For the word of God is living and powerful. (Hebrews 4:12, KJV)

The word of God is like a factory that manufactures results and programmes your life for steady success. This is a special revelation that God gave me during my aloneness with Him. Consequently this month has a special place in my salvation and ministry and now I am passing it to you with the hope that it will be a blessing to you. After the month of August the rest of the months beginning with September are what we call the *"Ember months*—embargo or governmental sanction months" in the spirit realm of reality. These months of the year prepare and determine the fate of many people. To some on the dark side it is a time of ungodly, bloody prosperity and affluence through the blood of innocent victims the world over - through plane crashes, shipwrecks, car accidents and many other means possible. Plans are also made to place strong, irrevocable and deadly limitations on people, places, nations, churches, families, businesses and economy even politics. It is also the spiritual season for the war of nations. This is why intercessors that could stand in the gap matter so much. During this period, those that will fail next year are being determined and marked out:

- Churches and ministries that will close, or go down
- Pastors and brethren that will die physically or spiritually (backsliding or becoming apostate)
- Nations where there will be war
- Marriages and homes fatalities

All are being short listed and the verdict passed with demonic legality. And many are ignorant of this reality.

The word August has been adopted ages ago as meaning *"surprise, sudden, unexpected"* thus, August Visitor. And truly there are those visitors of life that are unprepared for this kind of visitor (strange events, mysterious happenings). They take you by real surprise. The devil utilises this slogan to do great damaging business. But guess what? Our God is the "GOD OF GREAT SUPRISES" who can surprise all surprises that will dare stare at you or visit you. You can surprise man, but not God. He alone can surprise you. When the devil or an event surprises you, step aside and let God – the mighty unmovable mover, the unchangeable changer – step in. He is our heavy weight champion of righteousness in whom there is no variableness neither shadow of turning.

The month of August comes from the Latin word "Augustus," the first Roman Emperor. This was not his real name, but a title for who he was and for what the Romans expected of every man in such an office. The adjective form of it means venerable and imposing. The reign of such a Roman mantle bearer must be a flourishing period - literally. When applied to literature it must be refined and classical in style. As a venerator, he is entitled to deep respect on account of character, age and association. By imposition, he has to be impressive, and formidable – especially his appearance. He has to:

- Lay tax, duty and obligations.
- Enforce compliance.
- Take advantage of people and arrange things to his advantage, first, and then to his government that put him there.
- He has to impose unfair demands if that will suit his quest.

This spirit has been the dominant spiritual character of the month of August unless God gives you the revelation to turn it into your advantage. Otherwise you might be a victim of the forces of ember months unawares. That is why it is the spiritual month of release. By release we mean to set free, to liberate, to unfasten, to allow movement from a fix position, to make information or recording publicly available, and to issue a film for general exhibition, liberation from restriction, duty or difficulty. As a child of God, use this month to stand in the gap for your family, your church, community, nation, school, and whatever connects and concerns you. Free out souls, that are marked to die by air, land or sea or other means like war, crime or violence. Liberate the nation and communities from mayhem and bloodshed or wanton destruction. Unfasten people, finances, marriages that are in chains awaiting execution by the wicked world.

Even today many people are in bondage. So missionaries are led to difficult places, literally going through hell on Earth. Facilitate the free movement of good things into your country, village, town, your gates and cities. Look at what the Bible say about your gates – claim it and stand on it (Isa.60:1-5; 10-12). Read and meditate carefully on the words of the Prophet Isaiah:

> *6 "Is this not the fast that I have chosen: To loose the bonds of wickedness, To undo the heavy burdens, To let the oppressed go free, And that you break every yoke? ... 1 Arise, shine; For your light has come! And the glory of the Lord is risen upon you. 2 For behold, the darkness shall cover the earth, And deep darkness the people; But the Lord will arise over you, And His glory will be seen upon you. 3 The Gentiles shall come to your light, And kings to the brightness of your rising ... 10 "The sons of foreigners shall build up your walls, And their kings shall*

minister to you; For in My wrath I struck you, But in My favor I have had mercy on you. 11 Therefore your gates shall be open continually; They shall not be shut day or night, That men may bring to you the wealth of the Gentiles, And their kings in procession. 12 For the nation and kingdom which will not serve you shall perish, And those nations shall be utterly ruined. (Isaiah 58:6,60:1-3,10-12, NKJV)

Begin to release better things into your life, your home, family and spiritual positioning. Deal with all limitations. Learn from this example:

4 So it was, when I heard these words, that I sat down and wept, and mourned for many days; I was fasting and praying before the God of heaven. 5 And I said: "I pray, Lord God of heaven, O great and awesome God, You who keep Your covenant and mercy with those who love You and observe Your commandments, 6 please let Your ear be attentive and Your eyes open, that You may hear the prayer of Your servant which I pray before You now, day and night, for the children of Israel Your servants, and confess the sins of the children of Israel which we have sinned against You. Both my father's house and I have sinned. 7 We have acted very corruptly against You, and have not kept the commandments, the statutes, nor the ordinances which You commanded Your servant Moses. 8 Remember, I pray, the word that You commanded Your servant Moses, saying, 'If you are unfaithful, I will scatter you among the nations; 9 but if you return to Me, and keep My commandments and do them, though some of you were cast out to the farthest part of the heavens, yet I will gather them from there, and bring them to the place which I have chosen as a dwelling for My name.' 10 Now these are Your servants and Your people, whom You have redeemed by Your great power, and by Your strong hand. 11 O Lord, I pray, please let Your ear be attentive to the prayer of Your servant, and to the prayer of Your servants who desire to fear Your name; and let Your servant prosper this day, I pray, and grant him mercy in the sight of this man." For I was the king's cupbearer. (Nehemiah 1:4-11, NKJV)

Read also the example of Daniel and do the same. You will see tremendous result especially during midnight prayers or night fasting:

3 Then I set my face toward the Lord God to make request by prayer and supplications, with fasting, sackcloth, and ashes. 4 And I prayed to the Lord my God, and made confession ...19 O Lord, hear! O Lord, forgive! O Lord, listen and act! Do not delay for Your own sake, my God, for Your city and Your people are called by Your name. (Daniel 9:3-4,19, NKJV)

Learn from the example of Nehemiah and Daniel and make every August a time of release. Not only in interceding alone but use your mouth with the Scriptures to entreat the LORD for all that is in accord with His will. If you want to be more firmly guided on this release period, you can use the address at the end of this book to contact me and I will be glad to help you. You can request your copy of *The Month of Release Against Ember Months*. It is a valuable tool to equip you to be a victor and not a victim during those months. In the book of Joshua (1:8), your success depends largely on your continued meditations on the word of God. You have to be faithful to the word of God, meditate on it, talk about it and obey it fully.

We do not fight with physical weapons. Our weapons are not carnal, but mighty in God through Christ to dismantle like an old building every formation of darkness:

> *3 For though we walk in the flesh, we do not war according to the flesh. 4 For the weapons of our warfare are not carnal but mighty in God for pulling down strongholds, 5 casting down arguments and every high thing that exalts itself against the knowledge of God, bringing every thought into captivity to the obedience of Christ. (2 Corinthians 10:3-6, NKJV)*

Make sure your obedience to Christ is complete. Do not consider attacking Satan when you are not obeying Christ for he will deal with you roughly. Never speak anything that will be a hindrance to your spiritual victory. Let the word of God be your mirror and the law of perfect liberty – any other liberty is fake and damaging. Keep pondering God's word every morning as a man looking at the dressing mirror and accept the reflection it gives to you. Be ready to confront what it shows you for what you fail to confront you will never conquer. Be a doer of what you hear. If you are a preacher of the word, practice what you preach and then preach what you practice. This will bring eternal result and lasting peace with blessings that endure. Programme yourself for your future. Listen attentively to all messages in various programmes that you do attend, for it comes with the anointing of God to solve your problem. In turn, you can help solve others' problems for every one of us was created to solve a problem. Look for someone today to help solve their problems; in so doing you will be solving your own. As you adopt this as a lifestyle, you are programming yourself for enduring, godly success.

Chapter Nine
Choosing to Order Your Days

Literally, the day is the time between sunrise and sunset. It is a unit of time under 24 hours. The day has daylight, thus we say, *"as clear as day."* It has in it eight hours, the length of time in which work is normally done. It could mean a historical period – those *"good old days."* Day can also refer to the present time, the issues of the day. It can speak of the prime of a person's life: I have *"had my day,"* or *"in my day."* Or it can mean a future time: *"I will do it one day."* We talk of days for a specific festival or event - on my graduation day, on Christmas day. It can speak of a battle or contest: *"win the day."* We now talk of all in a day's work, the normal routine, at the end of the day when all is said and done, call it a day. That is end of a period of activity - day after day without respite.

Another definition follows that "DAY" means:

- A period of opportunity: *"He has made everything beautiful in its time." (Ecclesiastes 3:11, NKJV)* In His time, oh He is El De'a – the God of Knowledge – who made everything right, good, beautiful, and marvellous. What is His time? Your whole life time as a set of time for opportunity or opportunities. Akrogoniaios lithos our "Chief Cornerstone" has made all things pertaining to you in all spheres beautiful – hallelujah! (Ephesians 2:20; 1 Pet. 2:6; 1 Samuel 2:3; Proverbs 2:5; Daniel 1:17)

- A point or period in time: This is when you become more relevant to the world, your family, community, office and the church. A point in time when your good aroma can be noticed by all your neighbors. May El Ch'ay, the Living God, even the God of Life, bless you with good works! (Deut. 5:26; Josh. 3:10; 1 Sam. 17:26)

- A day assigned to a particular purpose or observance: Your life purpose is the quality of being determined to do or achieve something. How firm is your purpose? Your purpose is an anticipated outcome intended to guide your planned actions.

These are some of the uses of the word day in plain English. The meaning may vary depending on your regional English. Your day will determine your calendar and your year; the calendar will not determine your day in the name of Jesus Christ.

When you carefully study all of these entries and others, you will appreciate the fact that *day* has an important role in one's life from the day you were born to when you drop can be considered as one single day. *"A whole day's journey"* from the sun rise, when you were born, to the sun set, when you die in an extreme ripen golden old age (*not premature death or death by accident, plan crash or some attach by wicked satanic personalities*), the Bible says it must be praise -- yet not so for many people. Theirs is that of sorrows, afflictions and wreckage contrary to God's word. You have two principal days of note: the day you were born and the day you die. How you were born and how you die matters much. Every living person has three determining days that speak into your life strongly and without reservation:

1. Yesterday - your teacher or tutor
2. Today - your graduation day
3. Tomorrow - your set of opportunities

You can learn from history to bring diagnoses but you do not dwell on yesterday or in history. Today is very important and it is an irrefutable determining factor or parameter for tomorrow, if it will dare to be. It is called your graduation day. After graduating you look for work to put into practice what you have studied. From there you earn a living. Tomorrow never exists until you prepare a solid foundation for it to exist. But I pray that you see your tomorrow in good faith and favour in Jesus' name. Start now to arrange the way your bed will be, for you are the one to lay on it. Do not dress it up as if for rats, retired bingo or for sick people waiting to be thrown away. Do not pour raw acid on it. Do not hide it in thorns, time bombs or explosives and wickedness. You are the one who will lay on it. Do not murder yourself; God still loves you. Dare not to be wicked to yourself or any other person. Live as one created and loved by God. He asked me to tell you that He loves you. He called you beloved and His wish for you is far above all that you can imagine, far above what the enemy wishes against you (3 John 1:2).

We do say that the day shall tell. Each day has a story to tell. They speak revealing facts, good or evil, even secret activities. Oh, may your day speak good and not evil. May it speak well of you. May it favour you and not hate you. May an enemy not use your day to fight and speak evil against you. Look at what Job has to say:

> *7 I said, 'Age should speak, And multitude of years should teach wisdom.' 8 But there is a spirit in man, And the breath of the Almighty gives him understanding. 9 Great men are not always wise, Nor do the aged always understand justice. (Job 32:7-9, NKJV)*

Your *"days"* can teach you wisdom as well as foolishness, from agony and forbearance that presses you toward negative indulgence. Network providers have automated machines that whatever they want their customers to hear they can programme it into it. A prompt command responds to your call according to the wish of the masters. So are the days, years, weeks, months, morning, noon and nights. Every new day begins and ends at midnight when so many people are deep asleep, snoring, and dreaming of climbing mahogany trees and the Kilimanjaro Mountains. Blessed would you be called who will utilise that midnight hour to prophetically computerise instructions into your days, years, months and nights. As the new day rolls in and the old one flies away, tell your new day and morning what they should obey and speak as your defences against any other voice and programming. Command the day and morning, to obey your destiny in Christ. Open the Holy Pages; blow the written heavenly grammar to their hearing and bookmark it. Pin it to your taskbar, menu start bar and provide short cuts to your flight dashboard of the day. Do you understand? If you do not do this, sorry. Others will help you to your disadvantage.

> *7 Truly the light is sweet, And it is pleasant for the eyes to behold the sun; 8 But if a man lives many years And rejoices in them all, Yet let him remember the days of darkness, For they will be many. All that is coming is vanity. 9 Rejoice, O young man, in your youth, And let your heart cheer you in the days of your youth; Walk in the ways of your heart, And in the sight of your eyes; But know that for all these God will bring you into judgment. (Eccl.11: 7-9, NKJV)*

Here the sweet light and the sun points to the beauty of creation in one's life which covers every good thing that life can bring. But remember the *"days of darkness"* – days of afflictions, unforeseen circumstances, the death of all things, hardship – all are called the days of darkness. Many people, even though proclaiming Christ, are waylaying in it because they allow an idiot seated on a dirty evil mat to computerise their days, months and years while they are inside thick blankets. An enemy is busy dishing out instructions into their days, morning, years and nights when they are running after vanities, spending the night in night clubs, disco dancing, and watching movies. Jesus told a parable about a man who sowed good seed in his field. But while his men slept, an enemy came along and sowed weeds into his field (Matthew 13:24-25). A man's enemies can even be the men of his own house.

The Bible says that they are many such days of darkness. All come with vanity and emptiers to empty you through marital turbulence, police cases, court cases, hospitalizations, burglaries, bereavements and so on. Days of darkness are days of such wickedness that only God can keep you going. You labour to no profit and other people constantly reap your harvest. After building, you are sacked. You train them but they kill you. You say peace, peace while they shout war, war. You try to make yourself understood and acceptable but they insult, abuse and put you into debate. You spend hours studying but cannot pass the exam. At the edge of breakthrough, climbing story upon story, one after another, the list goes on but for how long will this be? When your blood is still hot, yet nothing cheers you up. You become an observer newspaper, looking at the world going and returning. You greet them when they go and when returning but who greets you? At best you become the latest anointed sermon of the day for baby food preachers and prophets.

Some will be bold to tell you, *"Brother, sister – you know I am a prophet and I love you. Search yourself."*

> *31 "O generation, see the word of the Lord! Have I been a wilderness to Israel, Or a land of darkness? [In life some are in this kind of condition but I want to cheer you up. Relax His wounded hands will touch you.] Why do My people say, 'We are lords; We will come no more to You'? 32 Can a virgin forget her ornaments, Or a bride her attire? Yet My people have forgotten Me days without number. (Jeremiah 2:31-32, NKJV)*

This is God lamenting because some gave the devil a place to fix an evil wardrobe. As you read this Scripture, stop and think: is this my classroom? If this resembles your attitude towards God then it will be difficult to come out of your dark days, even if you quote the entire Bible. Amend your ways and consider you latter end. Come to terms with God and acquaint yourself with Him and it shall be well with you.

> *21 "Now acquaint yourself with Him, and be at peace; Thereby good will come to you. 22 Receive, please, instruction from His mouth, And lay up His words in your heart. 23 If you return to the Almighty, you will be built up; You will remove iniquity far from your tents. 24 Then you will lay your gold in the dust, And the gold of Ophir among the stones of the brooks. 25 Yes, the Almighty will*

be your gold And your precious silver; 26 For then you will have your delight in the Almighty, And lift up your face to God. 27 You will make your prayer to Him, He will hear you, And you will pay your vows. 28 You will also declare a thing, And it will be established for you; So light will shine on your ways. 29 When they cast you down, and you say, 'Exaltation will come!' Then He will save the humble person. (Job.22:21-29, NKJV)

Why did I come forth from the womb to see labor and sorrow, That my days should be consumed with shame? (Jeremiah 20:18, NKJV)

Mark the phrase: *"my days should be consumed with shame?"* This is the mystery surrounding many people today. You might belong here. From Kindergarten to old age, wear and tear, life becomes bitter gall. *"I preach, sing and dance Jesus – God tell me, why me?"* The answer is that once you know your stand with your heavenly father is in good shape, stop lamenting, rise up, clean your eyes to see well, and say the right thing. Wake up at midnight and confront your days with the words of God not your own words. The devil does not fear prayer but the word of God. Prayer is not the strategy but it produces it. Your tongue carries enormous power than can quench many evil fires and floods. Rearrange the situation. Start now and you will give the testimony.

So Hezekiah said to Isaiah, "The word of the Lord which you have spoken is good!" For he said, "At least there will be peace and truth in my days." (Isaiah39:8, NKJV)

Let me give you the other good side of what Hezekiah said for there is a sense in every nonsense: "Well, my pastor, thank you for your rebuke and correction. I accept my fault. I did wrongly and what you say that the Lord said – you are my pastor. I may not doubt your anointing so, sir, the message is good. BUT I am standing on my toes in full assurance of what I know of my position with God as His child and as His object of mercy: 'IN MY DAYS THERE SHALL BE PEACE AND TRUTH.' Thank you, sir."

No matter what happen to others that you prophesy, no matter what people say about you, no matter your mistakes, Jesus died once for all your sins and mistakes – past, presence and future. You can no longer be held hostage by your mistakes. Give your past and present condition a graveyard burial, never to be resurrected against you, for His blood has atoned you and is now speaking on your behalf. Move forward into the future God has for you. Your tomorrow cannot be like yesterday nor be measured by your present state. What has happened, and where you come from will not determine where you are going. Your end cannot be predicted based on your beginnings. Where you start is not as important as where you will finish. You are going where you have never been, to create something you have never had, and to become what God had in mind in creating you. There are no mistakes, no experiences, no events, no men that can override God's decision concerning you, your life and your ministry. God has chosen to call you, to use you, to send you, and to work with you. He knows every mistake you will ever make, everything you will endure, everything that will happen to you.

In spite of these difficulties, in His manifold mercies, He chooses to lift you up to His glory. As the Bible notes, you will say also: *"The lines have fallen to me in pleasant places; Yes, I have a good inheritance." (Psalm 16:6, NKJV)* Therefore, "SIR, IN MY DAYS THERE SHALL BE PEACE AND TRUTH" TO THE SHAME OF THE DEVIL AND TO THE GLORY OF GOD, MY HEAVY WEIGHT CHAMPION OF RIGHTEOUSNESS IN WHOM THERE IS NO VARIATION, NEITHER SHADOW OF TURNING." When you think and speak like this, there is no way you will live a wrong life with God. It will keep you in tune and you will be able to pray and sing "In tune with Thee, in tune with Thee. Lord, keep my heart in tune with Thee, in tune with Thee."[1]

The steps of a good man are ordered by the Lord, And He delights in his way. (Psalm37:23, NKJV)

Not that the steps of God are ordered by the good man or that the steps of the good man are ordered by himself inviting God to endorse. But ordered by, monitored by, directed by, and programmed by the Lord. But when this good man has become spiritually lazy and falls asleep into thick blankets, and become less concerned, the enemy, the bad man, the devil will sow evil seeds into the good man's days and years against the good man's destiny. *"But while men slept, his enemy came and sowed tares among the wheat and went his way. (Matthew13:25, NKJV)* Do you want God to direct and establish your steps? Then, practice waking up early to command your morning, and your day. The inability of many decent Christians to understand this truth has resulted in their inability to control what happens to them and take possession of what belongs to them.

Understand how God works and discover your position in Christ. Realize that nothing happens to you by accident, chance or coincidence. There is a divine division of labour. God brings divine opportunities – your part is the responsibility to recognise and maximise each one of them. It becomes an imperative and an urgency for you to learn how to declare God's word into your day, every morning, before moving into the day's routine. Ward off every evil programmed into the day by agents and workers of wickedness. Invite the Holy Spirit to be your overseer and the power in charge. Say to yourself *"I am going to walk into my divine opportunities. I will be led by God into the right places and at the right time. My God is not a God of chance and fatalism. Nothing comes to me by chance for fatalism."* This is just a sample of what you should be confessing, for good confessing in faith changes things. Even if it delays, do not get discouraged – keep on that way as a life-pattern.

Never pretend, even a degree, to be what you are not. Remember the ugly fate of the sons of Scevas. The Bible called them vagabond, apprentice sorcerers for trying to do what they knew was wrong for them to try.

> *15 And the evil spirit answered and said, "Jesus I know, and Paul I know; but who are you?" 16 Then the man in whom the evil spirit was leaped on them, overpowered them, and prevailed against them, so that they fled out of that house naked and wounded. 17 This became known both to all Jews and Greeks dwelling in Ephesus; and fear fell on them all, and the name of the Lord Jesus was magnified. (Acts 19:15-17, NKJV)*

The demons saw through their gimmick and failure. They carefully examined the foolish young men, turning their eyes fearfully red: "You vagabonds, Jesus we know too well. Paul, thank God that it was not him who came but you, for we cannot stand his presence. It is hot devouring fire. Tell us who are you, trying to attempt what is not in your power and jurisdiction to do? Now has the battery exploded on you." (Act 19:15, paraphrased) It was a public display and reckless shame. Anything that does not concern you, do not get involved. You are not called to give an answer to every report that you hear. Stop using your ears for witch hunting. If they hire you, refuse the salary for it will purge you. Never demand the head of a prophet for your birthday celebration. If they give it to you would you be able to eat it? Why demand what is bigger than you, that which you can't chew? Ask your first cousin, Herod, and he will tell you that when men demand and accept the head of a prophet it will end their celebration at noon with the king of terror.

---

[1] *Perry, Juliette E. United Praise. The Lorenz Publishing Co. Copyright 1908. p. 151. Retrieved 8/2/2013 at http://www.hymnary.org/text/keep_thou_my_heart_in_tune_with.*

Chapter Ten
Choosing Who You Will Become

12 But as many as received Him, to them He gave the right to become children of God, to those who believe in His name: 13 who were born, not of blood, nor of the will of the flesh, nor of the will of man, but of God. (John 1:12-13, NKJV)

But as many who have, not who wish to, or are considering, but who have.....He gave the power to become the children of God. You don't struggle to be a child of God: *"Oh, I am struggling daily to be but it has not worked out. Maybe I should just keep trying or reconsider it later?"* Procrastination is a thief of time; doubt is a thief of courage; and unbelief is the mother of all evil. Stop trying and make up your mind now. What gives you the guarantee that tomorrow is there for you when you have no guarantee for the next minute?

To be born a male is a matter of birth, but to be a man is a matter of choice. The same could be said of a woman – that to be a female is a matter of birth but to become a woman of honour who can take charge even when men have become women and women become men, is a matter of choice. You could be a wonderful girl and a fair lady to be admired yet never become a woman of honour. You can become a fine boy and a nice guy yet fail to develop into a man all through life. It is not just a considerable choice, but a crucial choice in life. Starting today, I have made up my mind that this is who I want to be even if no one encourages me or buys my ideas. With God on my side, who or what can be against me! One with God is majority. Because He prevailed, I shall prevail. There may be delays and obstacles may rise, but because there is something about me and in me to be celebrated, I will make it, I am making it, I have made it. Yes, the Lord is on my side.

This is not just a lazy man's talk nor the random talk of a parrot when enticed with a peanut, or reading and repeating of a creed or some 4-step motivation speech or prayer as one chanting mantras. Rather, men develop ideas that could become a solid business, who have first chosen not to walk in the counsel of the ungodly, nor standing with the scornful (*addressing yourself to the distasteful expression of extreme contempt by people that suppress and trample the word of God underfoot and disdain Him publicly*), nor sitting in the seat of demolishers. Counsel is something that provides direction or advice as to a decision or course of action. But when counsel is given by the ungodly there is a problem. It is serious tragedy for the ungodly to give counsel and consolation to the godly. Who is your counsel – unbelievers, backsliders, the fallen away, Satan or the godly and the Holy Spirit? This is the language of winners and not of people with a victim mentality. They aim with a steady focus and activated convictions, making sure that no bullet is wasted. They target the unprotected forehead of their local and international Goliath. First, submit your life to Christ now if you haven't done so as your personal Lord and Saviour. Then you are qualified to be called a child of God. It will now be possible to receive the power of God to live and remain a child of God in a changing world of evil and deadly compromise. You will now begin to move daily into the very purpose for which God created you. In John 6:44, Jesus said that no man on his own effort can come to Him unless the Father has drawn the person to Him. By reason of new birth you have been drawn to Christ, you are immediately entitled to every blessing that comes with His death, resurrection and ascension. You do not need to write another application and fill the consultation forms with a seed faith to be considered.

> *He makes me to lie down in green pastures ... (Psalm 23:2, NKJV)*

God has the ability to prosper you, to bring calmness, peace and lasting joy and lead you to the land of your celebration. In the battle of the brave, the loser bows. It is the winner that will get the mandate. Must you die a struggling, suffering, wrecked, peaceless man without Christ? No, cease from your labour (Isa.30:15;

Rev.14:13; Matt.11:28) for there is rest for your weary soul. Lay down your life before Him. Say to Him:

Lord, here is my life. Use it for your glory. Lord Jesus, I have the confidence that you are more than able to make everything you have planned for me come to pass without fail. By you Lord Jesus, I shall live and not die. I shall be raptured and not go to hell, for it was not meant for me. Lord, I shall be fulfilled and content. In your hands my life is in safe keeping. Therefore I shall be green and vitalized. Yes Lord, I am persuaded that you are able to keep that which I have committed unto thee and you will establish me a holy person unto God. All my days shall be fulfilled – not one shall be taken away and neither shall I be robbed of my years nor be denied of my prime life. Thank you for being the resident of the seat of affection of my life. You are the centre of my life, both now and forever. In you I live and move. I am yours and yours will I always be. You are the reason for my being. Oh hallelujah!

There are a great number of people that would be more than happy to give you advice. Many of them do have your best interests at heart, and want the best for you. Then there are those who may wish to trip you up and mislead you. God knows this and, thankfully, He has given us His Word that we may know what counsel to heed and what to disregard (See 2 Tim. 3:16-17). To be able to know the difference and to follow it is a great blessing from God, and a skill that we should always seek to cultivate. Then we can be like the righteous Job, and strive to keep the counsel of the wicked far from us (Job 21:16. 22:18). As children of God, it is extremely important that we do not walk in the counsel of the ungodly. Following the wrong counsel brings with it severe consequences. In 1 Kings 12, Rehoboam sought counsel from the older men who had served his father and the younger men who were his peers. He refused the counsel and wisdom of the older men while choosing to follow the counsel of his peers. In so doing, the kingdom split and the greater part of the people followed Jeroboam as their new king. As a result, many of the people participated in pagan worship (1 Kings 12:25-30). Many others in Scripture suffered great consequences because they chose to follow ungodly counsel.

Do Not Let the World Define You – Define Yourself.

Life is a series of definitions but when the definition is done by an enemy, life becomes a series of defiance. To define means to decide upon or fix definitely, to determine the essential quality of a person or thing. So I ask – what defines you? This is a question you have no doubt been asked at some point in your life, directly or indirectly, by events, challenges or people. What determines your most essential quality? And you have probably never given much thought to this in your life. As stated in

Webster's Dictionary, the verb *"define"* means to identify the essential qualities or meaning of something. [1]

Finding the meaning of something might as well be considered the universal hobby of every human being but how may have truly found the meaning their lives deserve? How meaningful is your life and the things you keep pursuing? What are their eternal values and the eternal value of your life? What is your significance? What is that you are passionate about or what is your true passion in this single life given to you as gift by God? Where do you find fulfillment or what enthuses you? Be candid.

I earnestly believe that every situation and/or encounter has a specific purpose, no matter how insignificant or mundane it may appear. A situation will always present the opportunity to learn and, therefore, broaden your perspective. With glasses, your optical sense is corrected to bring that which is far or near into a perspective suited for *"perfect"* visibility. Now, everyone's view is different and defining what is perfect is determined through various tests: "A or B? What about now? Which one is better?"

Time and experience can impair our vision, causing things that once were clear and precise – like professional goals,

---

[1] *Merriam-Webster.com. Retrieved 8/28/2013 at http://www.merriam-webster.com/dictionary/define.*

relationships and love – to become blurred and uncertain. It is during these *"growing pains"* that we should utilize the opportunities to better ourselves and gain a more solid understanding of who we are, as opposed to stressing over situations out of our control. The one thing you do have control over is your reaction. Call it character building.

What we see in others is essentially a reflection of ourselves – our projections and prejudices. Anytime you judge someone, you reveal more about your own character than anything else. When you judge someone, you do not define them – you define yourself.

If You Do Not Know How To Be Who You Should Be, Then Choose To Be God's Choice.

God chooses obedient, faithful people for places of great responsibility. They may appear to be eccentric or downright strange on the outside (Elijah and John the Baptist were not *"normal"* people), but at their core, God sees something He can trust. He knows they are sold out for Him and Him alone. I place a demand on you now; be totally sold out to God so there is something in you that He can trust.

God is no respecter of persons (Acts 10:34). Any one of us can be God's choice – in that way you become who you should become today and tomorrow. He has more positions of greatness to pass out than He has people who are willing and able to fill them. The following steps will help any of us meet God's criteria and be His candidate for favour:

1. **Immerse yourself in the Word of God**: There is a pattern among God's great heroes of the past in how much time they spent reading the Bible. Many of them read nothing else. Ask God to speak to you through His Word. God is going to give you new revelation from it every time you read. His word will purify and renew your thought processes. Jesus said, *"You are already clean because of the word which I have spoken to you." (John 15:3)*

2. **Get the heart of God**: This can only be done by spending much time in His Presence through prayer, asking Him questions and listening for His answer, and again, through immersing yourself in His Word. The man or woman who pursues God will soon find that God is now pursuing him!

3. **Submit (make yourself accountable) to a Bible base local church leadership**: You cannot become God's man or woman for the hour if you are not connected with the local Church. If you are not already plugged into a Bible-

believing church, where the Presence of God is very real and satisfying, you need to find one. Establish a relationship with your pastor. Let him know you want to be discipled and accountable.

4. **Be a faithful servant in the smallest things**: Jesus said, *"He who is faithful in what is least is faithful also in much; and he who is unjust in what is least is unjust also in much ... And if you have not been faithful in what is another man's, who will give you what is your own?"* *(Luke 16:10, 12, NKJV)* Do you want to preach or teach? Do you have a prayer and healing ministry? Ask the pastor how you can serve. He may want you to clean the restrooms, work in the nursery, or help with the yard work. When you see a need, meet it. This might mean picking up the scrap of paper that someone else left behind, so that the sanctuary looks neat. No act of servant hood is too small to be beneath God's notice. As you are faithful to serve in small ways, God will see to it that you get to serve in larger ways as well.

5. **Be an abandoned giver**: If God does not own your money, He does not own you. How you use your wallet is an accurate gauge of how well God can use you in all of life. We are coming into a time in history when the tithe is not going to be the end-all of what God expects of His people

anymore. He wants it all at His disposal. Being an
abandoned giver goes far beyond money. We have to get
the money issue settled first but we also must learn to give
of our time. We must learn to give our love lavishly to
others, without expecting favours from them in return. We
have been bought at a very heavy price, and we do not
belong to ourselves anymore (I Corinthians 6:19, 20). Jesus
gave it all for us. He did it, knowing full well that not
everyone would appreciate His gift.

6. **Never worry about what someone else has in Christ**:
Peter got himself into trouble by having his eye on John's
relationship and position with Jesus. He was envious of
John. *"20 Then Peter, turning around, saw the disciple
whom Jesus loved following, who also had leaned on His
breast at the supper, and said, "Lord, who is the one who
betrays You?" 21 Peter, seeing him, said to Jesus, "But
Lord, what about this man?" 22 Jesus said to him, "If I
will that he remain till I come, what is that to you? You
follow Me." (John 21:20-22, NKJV)* Jesus had great
ministry plans for both Peter and John. They functioned
differently but each was vital to the Kingdom of Heaven.
And Jesus loved them both. We get into an awful lot of
trouble spiritually when we covet someone else's place of
ministry. God will give you what is rightfully yours when

He has prepared you. You do not need to strive with someone else, either inside of yourself or right out where everyone can see what you are doing. God has appropriate, satisfying things for you, if you will just wait for Him.

7. **Do not desire visibility**: The funny part about visible ministry is that God does not give it to those who want it. He gives it to those who initially would like to run from it. He gives it to those who prefer to serve Jesus quietly, without fanfare. If you want visibility, you are looking for the approval of men, rather than the approval of God. God cannot have that. He needs people who are focused on His agenda, not their own. Read what Jesus had to say about "*tooting your own horn*" in Matthew 6:1-18.

8. **Believe God for what He says**: There is no shortcut to being God's choice. It is going to take time for Him to mold you into the maturity you will need to handle a place of responsibility and authority. In the meantime, God will be watching to see if you patiently hang onto the promises and dreams He has given you. He wants to see if you will believe Him with all your heart, no matter how much time goes by. He wants to see if you will cherish His word to you. Abraham waited twenty-five years for his promised son Isaac to appear, and Hebrews says of him, ***"And so,***

after he had patiently endured, he obtained the promise."
(Hebrews 6:15, NKJV)

When you begin to notice God moving you into new places of responsibility, keep in mind that the road will not be easy. Whenever God puts a plan in place, there will be opposition because the devil does not like God's plans. The enemy often uses people as his agents to oppose the work of God. Just because you have determined not to be envious and competitive does not mean other people are going to treat you likewise! It is not easy to stay sweet when we experience criticism, especially from our brothers and sisters in Christ. If we keep our focus on Jesus, and look for Him to set the record straight in time, we will be able to handle the lack of love from those who do not want us to have the place God has given us. Peter sums up how we should behave if we are to be God's choice:

> *"5 ... all of you be submissive to one another, and be clothed with humility, for 'God resists the proud, But gives grace to the humble.' 6 Therefore humble yourselves under the mighty hand of God, that He may exalt you in due time, 7 casting all your care upon Him, for He cares for you." (I Peter 5:5-7, NKJV)*

CHOOSE WHO YOU WANT TO BECOME! DO IT OR IT WILL DO YOU!

Chapter Eleven
Choosing Your Foundation

My good friend and family member of the household of faith, today by the Apostolic mandate upon my life, I commend you, soul, spirit, and body, including your name, your shadow, your footprint on the sand of time, your family and business or ministry or career unto God and to the word of His grace (word of His prophesy). He is able to keep you, able to build you up, able to give you an inheritance among them who are born again unto the day you will stand before the bema seat of Christ for the judgment and reward of your faith and pilgrimage in the victorious name of Jesus Christ. Amen.

> *"So now, brethren, I commend you to God and to the word of His grace, which is able to build you up and give you an inheritance among all those who are sanctified." (Acts 20:32, NKJV)*

As God's servant, I am talking to you today about your soul with affection and concern. I am full of care over what will become of you. I direct you, my good friend, to look up to God with faith, and commend you to the word of God's grace – not only as the foundation of your hope and the fountain of your joy, but as the rule of your walking. Even the most advanced Christians are capable of growing, and will find the word of grace helps their growth. As those cannot be welcome guests to the Holy God who are unsanctified, so heaven would be no heaven to them. But to all who are born again, and on whom the image of God is renewed, it is sure, as almighty power and eternal truth, make it so.

The words you have been reading and shall be reading to the end of this book contain the prophecy of God concerning your destiny. Every word from the book of Genesis to the book of Revelation is the prophecy of God concerning His Son Jesus Christ for your wellbeing on earth and your life to come. Each word comes with grace and truth, fulfillment and demonstration, revealing the very image of God, His person and His mind for you. For your own good, therefore, I advise you to stand on them, take them more serious than anything else. Speak them as your words, and act on them and their principles to build a better foundation for your life than that of your parents and ancestors. Never use your customs nor the traditions of your fathers nor how you have been doing things in the past to interpret God's word. Do no harm to it but allow it to destroy every faulty foundation in you which you have been building that has failed to work because it was laid on man, and the tradition of the fathers. It was laid on the bones of the old prophets and on the ancient and modern seat of Moses. Aaron celebrated behind Uzziah's backyard bow room with men of unclean lips that denied Isaiah from seeing the glory of God any earlier. Thank God Uzziah passed away so that Isaiah could see God. Today, as you can, I beg of you, speak a prophetic word coined out from God's word until you can flow well. Link it up with our rabbinical route:

> *Then God blessed them, and God said to them, "Be fruitful and multiply; fill the earth and subdue it; have dominion over the fish of the sea, over the birds of the air, and over every living thing that moves on the earth." (Genesis 1:28, NKJV)*

Connect with our Fathers – Abraham, Isaac and Jacob, the prophets, the Apostles – and consolidate it with Christ's blood and the spirit of creation. Hear this and take it to heart down deep into your soul: the MAN, was made last of all the creatures. This was both an honour and a favour to you. Your humanity was made the same day that the beasts were made. Your body was made of the same earth as theirs. While you are in the body, you inhabit the same earth with them. God forbid that by indulging the body, and the desires of it, we should make ourselves like the beasts that perish! For you, oh MAN, were to be a creature different from all that had been previously made. Flesh and spirit, heaven and earth, must be put together in you. Speak as did Christ who began His earthly ministry saying:

> *1 The Spirit of the Lord God is upon Me, Because the Lord has anointed Me To preach good tidings to the poor;*

He has sent Me to heal the brokenhearted, To proclaim liberty to the captives, And the opening of the prison to those who are bound; 2 To proclaim the acceptable year of the Lord ... (Isaiah 61:1-2, NKJV)

Be that man who hears and do the word of God, so that your house (your life) will be built upon the Rock that never fails (Luke 6:48-49). You can equally choose to be that man who, though hearing but does nothing with it because of indulgence to the traditions of the fathers and the bones of the old prophets, meddles with the rough edge mundane ideas that negate the word of God. Your house (life) then rests entirely on quicksand. One storm is enough to blow it out. Buildings of any design require a corresponding foundation to carry it for years to come without being a hazardous trap. Decide what you want to be, and then start laying the solid foundation for it. Stop being satisfied with the status quo (average, mediocrity mentality). Average is an enemy that you should fight and kill. Do not permit him to decide your outcome in life. Take note of these choices: "I have not"... "I forget" .... "I reach forth" ... "I press forward" (Philippians 3:13-14, NKJV paraphrased by the author; cp 1 Corinthians 2:6-13).

Looking again at Isa.6:1-6, the prophet, standing outside the temple, sees the Divine Presence seated on the mercy-seat, raised over the Ark of the Covenant, between the cherubim and seraphim, and the Divine glory filled the whole temple. Today, in

THE POWER OF GOD'S WORD TO TRANSFORM YOUR LIFE

your life, begin to see God upon His throne at the centre of all you do. 41 These things Isaiah said when he saw His glory and spoke of Him. 42 Nevertheless even among the rulers many believed in Him, but because of the Pharisees they did not confess Him, lest they should be put out of the synagogue 43 for they loved the praise of men more than the praise of God. (John 12:41-43, NKJV) That Isaiah saw Christ's glory, and spoke of Him, is a full proof that our Saviour is God. In Christ Jesus, God is seated on a throne of grace. Through him the way into the holiest place is laid open for you if you believe and speak it. Let not the Far-to see and the Sad-to-See (Pharisees and Sadducees) hinder you from a strong relationship with Jesus. The praise of men is not for your utmost good; run from it now.

FROM VICTIM TO VICTOR

Chapter Twelve

Choosing Your Destiny

1 A soft answer turns away wrath, But a harsh word stirs up anger. 2 The tongue of the wise uses knowledge rightly, But the mouth of fools pours forth foolishness. 4 A wholesome tongue is a tree of life ... (Proverbs 15:1-2,4, NKJV)

- A right cause will be better pleaded with meekness than with passion. Nothing stirs up anger like grievous words.
- He that has knowledge is to use it aright, for the good of others.
- Secret sins, services, and sorrows, are under God's eye. This speaks comfort to saints, and terror to sinners.
- A good tongue is healing to wounded consciences, by comforting them; to sin-sick souls, by convincing them; and it reconciles parties at variance.

A soft answer (simple tender response, proper use of the tongue, a response from careful consideration) turns away wrath (destructive anger, flaying up easily) but grievous words stir up anger. A gentle tongue has healing power that develops into the status of fountain of life; the soul that has it becomes a tree of life. Genesis 2:9 talks about the tree of the knowledge of good and evil. In the realm of the spirit of reality, a tree speaks of human beings.

Inside of every human being is the tree of good and bad knowledge depending where one tunes his life.

> *9 knowing that Christ, having been raised from the dead, dies no more. Death no longer has dominion over Him. 10 For the death that He died, He died to sin once for all; but the life that He lives, He lives to God. 11 Likewise you also, reckon yourselves to be dead indeed to sin, but alive to God in Christ Jesus our Lord.12 Therefore do not let sin reign in your mortal body, that you should obey it in its lusts. 13 And do not present your members as instruments of unrighteousness to sin, but present yourselves to God as being alive from the dead, and your members as instruments of righteousness to God. 14 For sin shall not have dominion over you, for you are not under law but under grace. (Romans 6:9-14, NKJV)*

The most hideous sin is committed with the mouth. For example:

1. Lying – a deadly sin (Proverbs 12:22)

2. Sowing discord (Proverbs 6:14,15)

3. Gossip – spreading intimate rumors of facts (Proverbs 20:19)

4. Slander – false reports about someone (Proverbs 10:18)

5. Tale-bearing – revealing secrets when you have no authority to do so. Knowing someone's fault is power. Character is having power and using it wisely (Proverbs 11:13)

6. Cursing – (Psalm 109:17-19)

7. Blasphemy – using God's name in a self-serving or profane way (Exodus 20:7; Leviticus 19:12)

8. Filthy language – expressing disrespect for God or for something sacred (Colossians 3:8)

9. Contentious speech- hurtful, or argumentative; involving or likely to cause controversy; inclined or showing an inclination to dispute or disagree; to engage in law suits (Proverbs.21:9)

10. Unbelief – negativity; rejection of a helpful and legitimate belief system (Hebrews 3:12)

Many destinies have been wasted, crushed, jailed, hamstrung, jammed, sold and destroyed by the wrong use of words and wrong choice of words. The tongue is that part of man – regardless of whether one is a man or woman, big or small, old or young – that gets them into the most trouble. An appendage as small as it is helps send many in the wrong direction and is responsible for many things the owner regrets over the long run. It is the most difficult to manage part of everyone's anatomy (Jas.3:3-5).

When your tongue is controlled, it can become a blessing to God and man. Uncontrolled it can compel you to think about how to control other people's lives (James 3:5-12). May I, like Matthew Henry, caution you not to give yourself the air of teachers, imposers and judges, but rather speak with the humility and spirit of learners. Do not censure one another, as if all must be brought to your standard.

If you live your life to obey Satan and his propaganda, to do evil things, then it shows that the tree in you produces evil knowledge. If Christ is counting gain from your heart and your life becomes a reward of His death and suffering on the cross, the tree in you produces good knowledge. The rigidly righteous is a tree of life. Be honest with yourself. Who is your father and master – Satan the devil or Christ the Lord and King? The two of them cannot share you and constantly fight to see who will win. That is why we have two kinds of tongues: the serpent tongue and the Holy Spirit tongue. The former brings death, even in relationships, with unruly evil and sets cities in infernos, corrupts nations, and entices leaders into the spirit of Nimrod (*the spirit of greed and witchcraft*). The latter is anointed to produce life and good waters for thirsty ones to drink – clean neat water not from bore holes. The Holy Spirit tongue is life changing for wholesome hearts.

The Holy Spirit inspired tongue brings life. It is a clean fountain. Adam being allured, incurved and overpowered by bedroom power (*lovey-lovey pastors and brethren*), yielded to operate solely by the strength of the former, the serpent tongue. By the "*Love me. I kiss you or we separate now – put the Bible down first and kiss me!"* game, Adam and Eve ate and died. That was the extent of their personal deliberate choice. Ironically, they became born again from life to death. Thank God that today in Christ Jesus we are sincerely born again from death to life. From paradise lost to paradise regained, praise God and never to go back to the former again (Rom.4:18-22, Jn.1:15-17).

The truth remains, however, that what we blamed Adam and his wife for doing is still being endorsed and practiced by many today. The fall of man is ongoing just as the redemption of man continues through our tangible choices. Choose the fall and many generations will go along with you. Choose redemption and many generations will follow suit. There is a revelation tie between knowing, believing and speaking. What you know is what you believe and speak. It has a finality power of conclusions, to put your life in shape or out of shape. It has the potential of making your life empty or full. Be careful, therefore, to get your tongue evaluated, circumcised and salted. Put it in good health by visiting the soul and destiny clinic (*Bible standard church or ministry, not free moral centres*) nearest to you. Tell the doctor there (*pastor*) to put you in the theatre and circumcise your tongue or do a surgical operation on your tongue to save many generations yet unborn. When you bring down one woman, generations are down. When you down one man, a whole posterity is gone.

If being downstream is your story today, then I ask you: who brought or is bringing you down? Joseph was brought down by his brethren but who brought you down and sold you to Egyptian merchants? And who will you be busy bringing down or have brought down already? Permit me to share the type of painful bitter truth you would not like to hear. Study the Bible closely – there is no atonement for the serpent tongue, only judgment. So where are you going on your own? If you think nothing of yourself, then think of others that are wounded, bruised, jailed, have become wedged and unworkable, damned, halted, buried, destroyed, separated, hunted and crushed by your severe shortage.

> *16 These six things the Lord hates, Yes, seven are an abomination to Him: 17 A proud look, A lying tongue, Hands that shed innocent blood, 18 A heart that devises wicked plans, Feet that are swift in running to evil, 19 A false witness who speaks lies, And one who sows discord among brethren. (Proverbs 6:16-19, NKJV)*

Your serpent tongue is a bulldozer (like a powerful tractor with a large blade in front to flatten areas the grounds of human destiny). The Bible gives many examples; here are just a few:

> *But he who repeats a matter separates friends. (Proverbs 17:9, NKJV)*

> *There is one who speaks like the piercings of a sword. (Proverbs 12:18, NKJV)*

12 A worthless person, a wicked man, Walks with a perverse mouth; 13 He winks with his eyes, He shuffles his feet, He points with his fingers; 14 Perversity is in his heart, He devises evil continually, He sows discord. 15 Therefore his calamity shall come suddenly; Suddenly he shall be broken without remedy. 16 These six things the Lord hates, Yes, seven are an abomination to Him: 17 A proud look, A lying tongue, Hands that shed innocent blood, 18 A heart that devises wicked plans, Feet that are swift in running to evil, 19 A false witness who speaks lies, And one who sows discord among brethren. (Proverbs 6:12-19, NKJV)

Have a close study of the writings of Jude from verses 5-12 and ask yourself: what do I gain in operating with the serpent tongue? One gossip in a church fellowship is enough to put the sign board of judgment: *"Ichabod ... 'The glory has departed from Israel!'"* (1 Samuel 4:21, NKJV)

5 But I want to remind you, though you once knew this, that the Lord, having saved the people out of the land of Egypt, afterward destroyed those who did not believe. 6 And the angels who did not keep their proper domain, but left their own abode, He has reserved in everlasting chains under darkness for the judgment of the great day; 7 as Sodom and Gomorrah, and the cities around them in a similar manner to these, having given themselves over to sexual immorality and gone after strange flesh, are set forth as an example, suffering the vengeance of eternal fire. 8 Likewise also these dreamers defile the flesh, reject authority, and speak evil of dignitaries. 9 Yet Michael the archangel, in contending with the devil, when he disputed about the body of Moses, dared not bring against him a

183

reviling accusation, but said, "The Lord rebuke you!" 10 But these speak evil of whatever they do not know; and whatever they know naturally, like brute beasts, in these things they corrupt themselves. 11 Woe to them! For they have gone in the way of Cain, have run greedily in the error of Balaam for profit, and perished in the rebellion of Korah. 12 These are spots in your love feasts, while they feast with you without fear, serving only themselves. They are clouds without water, carried about[c] by the winds; late autumn trees without fruit, twice dead, pulled up by the roots; 13 raging waves of the sea, foaming up their own shame; wandering stars for whom is reserved the blackness of darkness forever. (Jude 1:5-12, NKJV)

Let us have a little study of this all important Epistle, focusing on verses 5-6.

But I want to remind you, though you once knew this, that the Lord, having saved the people out of the land of Egypt, afterward destroyed those who did not believe. (Jude 1:5, NKJV)

SAVED BUT DESTROYED – Who is the person the Holy Spirit is pinching here? With trembling and hot tears flowing down my cheeks, I do not know – brother, sister, fellow pastor no matter your international airfield title – what is it that is arranging you for this kind of condition, having been saved you are destroyed at last? Having won men's applause and kingdoms, Lucifer will one day stare at your face, fix his eyes on you, and say, "*So, you will later come here?*" Some will wear a rainy season cap and say, "*But eternal security...*" What eternal security do you deserve when you have separated yourself from the faith, when you have jumped the fence and escaped from the boundary of the holy blood of Jesus Christ?

"I want" (v. 5): Jude expresses the burden of wanting desperately to warn his readers as I am doing now. He sees Old Testament examples as extremely important for Christians (see Rom. 15:4; 1 Cor. 10-11). The writer of Hebrews expands greatly on a similar insight regarding Israel's demise in the wilderness [the demise of the very church Christ died for in the world] (Num. 14: 28-35).

"Saved ... destroyed": In Hebrews 3:16-19, God miraculously delivered the nation of Israel out of Egyptian bondage (Exodus 12:51; Deuteronomy 4:34) only to have them respond in unbelief, doubting, and defecting from faith in God that He could bring them into the Promised Land (Numbers13:25-14:4), even to the extent of worshipping an idol of their own making, as well as murmuring against God instead of adoring Him. Ah! 99% of global pastors (better call parcels, big-shops, bush and beast shops not worthy of being addressed as Bishops, profane not prophets, tissues not more teachers, apostate unfit to be Apostles, ever-jivers not qualified as Evangelist) have with impunity introduced us to new idols of both ours and theirs with doctrines of internationalism – the old Nebuchadnezzar graduate school

(Exodus 16:7-12; 1 Cor. 10:10-11). That apostate generation died during 38 years of wilderness wanderings. And we are in the days of modern religious wanderings and Bible poverty in the wilderness of witting sin (Numbers 14:22-30, 35).

He is reminding them that just because they were saved, it does not mean they can do anything they choose, and still come to salvation. He is giving, as an example, the Israelites (God's people) whom He delivered from Egypt (the world).

They were delivered, but started complaining and doubting that God would take them to the Promised Land. God made them wander in the wilderness for 40 years until those who had doubted died. My friend, you cannot sleep on Delilah's lap and wake up in heaven. No, you cannot drink from the same cup as Pharaoh and swim in the religiotic-ocean of modern-day Sodom and Gomorrah, dancing at the gate of death to please Nebuchadnezzar and think that you will have a red-carpet reception in heaven.

Without faith it is impossible (*Not capable of occurring or being accomplished or dealt with*) to please God. It does not matter whether it is the Israelites on their way to their Promised Land, or believers in Christ who are on their way to their Promised Land. We do know there will be some, who stand before Jesus on judgment day, who will profess to be Christians, whom Jesus will tell to get away from Me, I never knew you (Matthew 7:21-23). We must walk in the salvation we receive to inherit heaven. It was *"those who did not believe"* (Jude 1:5, NKJV) who were *"destroyed."* Our faith (*the word of God we claim to know and preach*) in Jesus name, let it be the type that will save us at the end of the tunnel.

> *And the angels who did not keep their proper domain, but left their own abode, He has reserved in everlasting chains under darkness for the judgment of the great day. (Jude 1:6, NKJV)*

"Angels who did not keep" – This apostasy of fallen angels is described in Gen. 6:1-3 as possessing men who then cohabited with women. These angels, *"did not keep their proper domain,"* (*how many among professing believers have left their domain today*) i.e., they entered men who promiscuously cohabited with cheap market-place women, even their daughters. Apparently this is a reference to the fallen angels (*reference today people*) of Gen. 6 (*sons and daughters of God today*):

1. Before the flood, (2 Peter 2:5; Gen. 6:1-3) who left their normal state and lusted after women

2. Before the destruction of Sodom and Gomorrah (2 Peter 2:6; Gen. 19).

The transition to Sodom and Gomorrah in Jude 1:7 points to the similitude of the sin of homosexual acts and what these angels did in Genesis 6.

"The judgment of the great day" – The angels who sinned (*fallen angels*) are currently imprisoned and destined to continue in everlasting chains through the final judgment, when all demons and Satan are forever consigned to the *"lake of fire"* (Revelation 20:10, NKJV, also Matthew 25:41) prepared for them and all the ungodly (Rev. 20:15).

The word *"keep"* in the verse above is *"tereo"*, which means to guard, or keep an eye upon. The word *"reserved"* is translated from the same word that was translated *"keep"* in the verse above.

There are two archangels in heaven: Lucifer and Michael. Each of them had a position over the other angels. The possible reason there were one third following Lucifer is because they were under his command. When they chose to follow Lucifer, who is now known as Satan or the devil, they gave up their freedom of movement and are only allowed to minister when sent on an evil mission.

Demons, as we call them, or devil spirits as the Bible calls them, are still ministering spirits and abounding daily in large number. The influx is high behind the pulpit, pig playing and devouring on God's pallor. They just minister evil instead of good. We are bought and paid for by Jesus and we are His and must remain His. He alone can determine what can happen to us, not the devil.

They are waiting for the judgment of God (*maybe including you*), as is all intelligence. The chains, in the verse above are not literal chains, but a control over them. Notice this is not a literal place they are held, but they are dwelling in darkness. Many we see in the preaching industry today and their boosters we mourn and sing and declare them to be with Lord – but they are held in chains like wild beasts in iron caves waiting what befits them. The main thing we are to see in this is the fact that they fell after they had direct knowledge of God's existence and His throne.

You are entitled to love all pastors or leaders or constituted authorities. But if do not wish to love that pastor, or that you feel you no longer want to love or continue with him, you should not vent your mouth like a drone predator against him or her no matter your authentication. Whether by prayer, prophecy, vision or revelation, when you think *"After all, I am PASTOR UNIVERSE so I have an anointing to be a demolisher and a graduate of the*

'Accuser of the Brethren College of Science and Technology. '" You may succeed today but friend, sorry, stop wasting your time – you will never enter heaven. A sinner is not a Christian and a Christian does not continually practice sin. And all unrighteousness is sin. It is not for you so that you will not spoil it with the same vein. There is no atonement for you and your grandfather-in-business, Lucifer.

Some of you have wicked satanic anointing to sow, pray, and prophecy evil into people's minds and it germinates and abounds destructively. They hear and believe without investigation. Both you and your hearers have no place in the Heaven of Christ except in the destruction reserved for you and Lucifer. ***"Who are you to judge another's servant? To his own master he stands or falls. Indeed, he will be made to stand, for God is able to make him stand. (Romans 14:4, NKJV)*** The key question here is *"Who are you?"* God is asking you to give your identity and credential to qualify you to assume such a post in His kingdom which He will never assign to you.

> *10 Humble yourselves in the sight of the Lord, and He will lift you up. 11 Do not speak evil of one another, brethren. He who speaks evil of a brother and judges his brother, speaks evil of the law and judges the law. But if you judge the law, you are not a doer of the law but a judge. 12 There is one Lawgiver, who is able to save and to destroy. Who are you to judge another? (James 4:10-12, NKJV)*

The same question is being asked here – that we have only one Lawgiver and Judge. So when were you given this appointment without the Sanctum above knowing? Read meditatively the following passages - 1 Peter 2:1-3; Matthew 7:1-10,28; Proverbs 30:10-17 – and allow God's word to speak to you so that you will withdraw yourself from the forbidden grounds lest they kill you at the later end. Your success is not reckoned as success in God's eyes.

> *10 Do not malign a servant to his master, Lest he curse you, and you be found guilty. 11 There is a generation that curses its father, And does not bless its mother. 12 There is a generation that is pure in its own eyes, Yet is not washed from its filthiness. 13 There is a generation— oh, how lofty are their eyes! And their eyelids are lifted up. 14 There is a generation whose teeth are like swords, And whose fangs are like knives, To devour the poor from off the earth, And the needy from among men. 15 The leech has two daughters— Give and Give! There are three things that are never satisfied, Four never say, "Enough!": 16 The grave, The barren womb, The earth that is not satisfied with water— And the fire never says, "Enough!" 17 The eye that mocks his father, And scorns obedience to his mother, The ravens of the valley will pick it out, And the young eagles will eat it. (Proverbs 30:10-17, NKJV)*

If these scriptures describe you, bring your full and sincere repentance before the Lord now before there is no more time for you to find His favour and compassion.

To accuse in Scripture means the same as a legal accusation – as to a judge by a magistrate in a court of Law. It means:

1.   To give or charge someone of something evil
2.   To establish a case or cause against someone
3.   To lodge a complaint against someone
4.   To slander someone against his favour
5.   Publicly speaking or writing against
6.   A decision you have taken against someone, inviting others to propel it explicitly
7.   To throw a verbal assault on someone
8.   To forward yourself as an accuser against someone or something
9.   To call in an account against someone
10. To insult, treat, abuse, despite, to witness against somebody with intention to stop help from coming the person.

To one who destroys someone and all relationships that have a connection with the person, God the Holy Spirit now asks you, "Who are you to do this to even one soul for whom Christ died? Who are you to designate yourself as a malignant informer (for whisperers separate chief friends – Proverbs 16:28; Genesis 2:9; Revelation 2:7; 22:14,19)?" Talk about the tree of the "experience of blessing and calamity." By your choice, you can become the tree of blessing or of calamity depending on which tree you decide to eat of its fruits.

A wholesome tongue is a tree of life. (Proverbs 15:4, NKJV)

The tree of death, therefore, is not a wholesome tongue. Choose your own kind of tree, either to have that of life and blessings, or that of calamity and death. The reward will return on your head and your children up to the fourth generation. The CHOICE IS YOURS.

FROM VICTIM TO VICTOR

Conclusion

Choosing God's Best For Your Life

Judgment can be delayed, but not forgotten. God is righteous and does no injustice. He remembered the kindness of the Kenites, and the injuries that the ancestors of the Amalekites did to His people. How dangerous to be found among God's enemies. It is your duty to come out from among them lest you share in their sins and plagues (Rev.18:4).

Your mouth shows your conduct, whether that of a proud rebellious spirit or of a humble and perfect obedience spirit. King Saul destroyed only the refuse that was good for little. You are demanded to destroy that which could be sacrificed to the justice of God.

Your mouth can witness against you just as the noise of the cattle witnessed against Saul (1 Samuel 15:10-23). Your mouth could show your vain boasting of obedience to God and reveal your stern indulgence to the flesh. You love the world's entrees and unkind spirit, and neglect the holy duties which witness against you before God daily.

FROM VICTIM TO VICTOR

The best evidence of our being predestinated to the kingdom of glory, is our being sealed with the spirit of promise (Ephesians 1:13-14), and experience of the work of grace in our own hearts which should be the fruits of what we say to ourselves and others who daily listen to us:

> *11 For the grace of God that brings salvation has appeared to all men, 12 teaching us that, denying ungodliness and worldly lusts, we should live soberly, righteously, and godly in the present age, 13 looking for the blessed hope and glorious appearing of our great God and Savior Jesus Christ, 14 who gave Himself for us, that He might redeem us from every lawless deed and purify for Himself His own special people, zealous for good works. 15 Speak these things, exhort, and rebuke with all authority. Let no one despise you. (Titus 2:11-15, NKJV)*

In 1 Samuel 16:6-23, Saul made himself a terror. So the spirit of the Lord departed from him and an evil spirit filled the vacuum. If God and His grace do not rule us and our mouth, sin and Satan will have possession of us. The devil, by the divine permission, troubled and terrified Saul in the corrupt humours of his body and passions of his mind. Your passion can chart the course of your of life. Discover yourself and recover your destiny. King Saul grew fretful, peevish and discontented, and at times a madman. Your passion can reveal God's will for your life or quench it. Identify your passion to discover where your road is leading.

Your mouth is a powerful gate that sees much traffic. You are the doorkeeper. As you open it for traffic flow, unchecked traffic will either kill you or keep you alive. It can draw you nearer to God or drive you away from Him. It can steer you close to death or guard your life. Check the flow of your word traffic now to avert God's final axe.

May I encourage you in the Lord, you who have many times been inflicted with wounds and irreversible injuries, you who have been broken, killed and wounded many times by the grim swords in men's mouth filled with satiric knives that have caustically destroyed many souls. Destroyed servant of God, relatives and whomever passes through their mitotic corridors, His wounds, by the cruel peril hands of the Romans, will vindicate you, fight for you and heal your wounds. Christ will put a lasting smile on your face for he who laughs last, laughs best. David, your kinsman cousin at length, was pitched upon. He was the youngest of the sons of Jesse. His name signifies *"Beloved."* He was a type of God's beloved Son. What you are passing through now will drag you out of the bush to the palace of honour and glory. David was the least set of all the sons of Jesse but the spirit of the Lord came upon him. From that day forward, the pages of the ledger were changed. His anointing was not an empty ceremony, but a *"Divine"* celebration and power went with him as an instituted sign. He found himself advancing in wisdom and courage, with all

197

the qualifications of a prince, though not advancing in his outward circumstances. I do not know to whom am talking, but I think it is you. That satisfied David that his election was of God. My friend, it is all right. Wash your face and lift up your countenance; receive the decoration of a prince and move into your hall of fame. I release you out from every grave, every prison, every circumstance into your destiny of design and beauty. Begin to enjoy the perfect will of God for your life.

Let us go in again. Your mouth can also reveal to all men what evil, covetous root or righteous root from which your life arose, and show what sinfulness of sin or goodness of righteousness is manifested in you. When you say, *"I am sorry,"* you are only painting the book with kindergarten saliva, a true picture of hypocrisy and the fanfare repentance of a fool. You speak to show how anxious you are for people to stand right in your opinion and grant you their favour when in essence you have decided against God's opinion over your life and His glory and true favour.

When Saul spared Agag, he thought that the bitterness of death was past when it had not yet arrived. Agag, like some men today, tried to put off the evil day until Samuel (indeed God) called Agag to account for his sins. He justly made him suffer the example of his ancestors' cruelty; therefore was all the righteous blood by Amalek required.

You may be unconcerned now at the token of God's displeasure which you are under. I weep and mourn for you like Samuel over Saul day and night in my prayers. You are carnally secured by your Pharaoh and Nebuchadnezzar, operating in the frequency of Sodom and Gomorrah with a menacing mouth. Just as Christ wept over Jerusalem, He desires that you repent and change and do the will of God while it is day. Turn to Him not in form and appearance, but with earnest and deepest sincerity. Are you doing that now? Delay will be grave. If you fail, just like your grandfather Papa-Saul, from the very corridors of hell and Lucifer, evil spirit will not only trouble you but will invite you to your grave – God has spoken not me.

It is not just appearances, but that you have grown so wicked that you no longer feel guilty of anything. Like Boar, your heart pumps from behind as such when you see others with joyful respect to God trembling at the coming of your pastor, your leader, your father, that man or women of God – Oh that leader, you saturninely choose to stand taller than your shadows like an evil weed in the market place of Satan and the land of the dead, to use your sarcastic gateway (mouth) to destroy him or her, to run him down and force his ministry to close. Why do you choose to lock a man's door when he is still alive? Why do you think you can roof a house that is still being built? Why do want to place a ceiling when the roofing has not yet been completed?

With your words you kill and demand the head of the prophet who came peacefully to make sacrifices. Even God is weeping for all His prophets, His children killed and swallowed up by people of your kind. A curse hangs over your head and posterity, except you repent now and amend your ways considering your later end. I counsel with you today, switch off the ignition and possibly idle the engine. Go now and put things right. A child is not justified before his father for there are authorities the father possesses which he does not have above his father for life. Look for that man or woman of God, that leader or your own father and mother while they are still around, and ask for forgiveness. This may sound strange for you hearing that God is disappointed in you no matter your claims as you stand by your actions as justifiable. He is regretting having made you. Yes, your countenance and stature, your eloquence and skill have recommended you before men, even your accolades. Yet get this fact straight: that men can tell how you look, but God alone tells what you are. He judges men by the heart and, from there, He measures their height. Men often form a mistaken judgment of characters, but the Lord values only the faith, fear, and love, which are planted in the heart beyond human's discernment.

- Stop your campaign of mockery.
- Stop being a mimicker.
- Stop behaving as a victim displayed in the market for sale.
- Stop being a threat and trap setter, it will with time boomerang for time tells all events.

Behold, God standing by the entrance of the city beckoning you to come; respond now and tomorrow you will be a celebrity to Him

24 "The Lord bless you and keep you; 25 The Lord make His face shine upon you, And be gracious to you; 26 The Lord lift up His countenance upon you, And give you peace."' (Numbers 6:24-26, NKJV)

May the Lord answer you in the day of trouble! May the name of the God of Jacob set you securely on high! May He send you help from His sanctuary and support you from this day forward! May He grant your heart's desire and fulfill all your godly petitions. May time bring favour to you. From today your gate shall not be closed, neither day nor night, that good things will always rush into you habitation. Get connected to people that can carry your dream. Go forward in life and get appointed where you were disappointed. Generations shall honour God in you. You are a child of destiny. Have an enviable destiny. Discover yourself to recover your destiny. Men will see your glory and come to your light in the mighty name of Jesus Christ! Let the boldness of the wicked in their mischievous course animate and embolden you in a pious course in Jesus' name! Amen!

If you are not born again by God's Spirit, do not pretend, it kills, it is void, and there is no gain in that course. Where you are, I ask you to invite the LORD Jesus into your heart so that the prophetic utterances in this book will work for you. Entrust yourself to the LORD first before praying the prayers below. Wherever the Holy Spirit has convicted you of something as you journey through this book, repent from it and receive God's forgiveness. Use the address at the end to write to me for any spiritual help that you need from me. Ask reasonable questions or send your comments as well. Tell me what God has done to you as you read this book. You can also connect with me through Facebook and other links. You can also extend invitations to me to minister God's riches to your church, ministry or group. You will be glad you did and your people will be blessed. If you need online leadership training, networking in Apostolic and intercessors network, then please write requesting details. I believe you have learned many precious truths that will turn your life into eternal blessings within your generation. Any area the Holy Spirit has directly or otherwise ministered to you, confront it and follow these prayers to expand your personal prayers. You will find great reward for choosing to do so. Start with confession, then praise and worship. Call on the name of Jesus Christ 3Xs, the blood of Jesus Christ 3Xs, the fire of God 3Xs and then begin to prayer.

1. *Dear heavenly Father, I have set watch before my mouth to keep the door of my lips. I thank You for You have given me wisdom and understanding to speak words that are in agreement with your plans and purposes for my life in the mighty name of Jesus Christ. Amen.*

2. *Eternal Loving Father, I thank you for bringing your word alive into my spirit and filling me with your Spirit and wisdom and revelation so that I may grow up strong and rooted in your word, in the glorious name of Jesus Christ. Amen.*

3. *Precious and Loving Father, today I have chosen to set a strong watch over my mouth to speak nothing but your words of grace and voice your thoughts alone. Teach me to discipline my tongue to speak words that are in line with your provisions for me in Christ Jesus. Amen.*

4. *Dear Father, Your word is precious to me and I daily long for it as a newborn baby longs for its mother's milk. It fills me with Your wisdom and understanding, to face my world and cause word-based changes in the name of Jesus Christ. Amen.*

5. *Father Lord, I confess that I am not a child of chance. God has prearranged my life for good and not for evil to give me hope and a future. I walk in those paths that have been laid out for me before the foundations of the world and I prosper in all my ways, in the conquering name of Jesus Christ. Amen.*

6. *My Father, thank you for the power to become Your child indeed and for all the wonderful rights and privileges that accrued me because I am born of*

You. I am fully convinced that I will live to fulfil my destiny in You, for You are the one working in me that I may be all that You have ordained for me to be in the powerful name of Jesus Christ. Amen.

7. *Father God, I thank You for making me wise and guiding me by Your wisdom to dig my foundation deep in the Rock which is Christ. By this, I can outlast every storm that is in the world in the name of Jesus Christ. Amen.*

8. *My heavenly Father, thank You for the changes that are taking place in me now, for I have kept Your word before my eyes always and I am changed by the Spirit of God to conform to Your word in the victorious name of Jesus Christ. Amen.*

9. *Oh Lord God, King of my soul, You have anointed my tongue with power, and given me wisdom to speak Your word that will direct my feet in the path You chose for me in the name of Jesus Christ. Amen.*

10. *Lord God, I confess that I am the righteousness of God in Christ Jesus! That I am a true representative of the Creator of the universe. Therefore, I rule and reign in this life over every circumstance I face. I confess that from today my life has been anointed to speak words of grace and compassion and love. Amen.*

11. *My tongue as my own tree of life is reserved to build souls and my destiny, even my posterity. Amen and Amen.*

Epilogue

If the Lord has blessed you through this book, write to me today. This will encourage me to do more. For prayers and counselling, for Bible correspondence and online Bible College training, contact me today through:

HealingAfrica@Hotmail.com

About the Author

Apostle Prof. Livingstone David Covenant is a missionary to the African nations - called to bring the gospel to the nations. His ministry is simply an attempt to obey God and encourage others to do so. He gave his life to Jesus Christ as his personal Lord and Savior at the tender age of five years. Six months later he started preaching the gospel till today with the Lord's backing. He became a full-time missionary for Christ on August 14th 1968 during the Nigerian civil war. He is now a Bishop by position and an Apostle of the CROSS by calling. He founded the Africa Divinity College of Missions to provide pastoral education and leadership training. The Lord has used Apostle Livingstone in the training of African Leaders in a distinctive, instinctive manner that is rarely found in any other African Leadership Colleges. More than 2,000 people of God have been trained through correspondence and another 1,500 through college programmes. Roughly 200 children that have made mistakes, been rejected and abandoned have been trained at the different levels and skills.

WordTruth Press℠

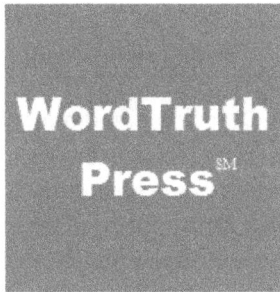

Quality resources with significant spiritual impact

On the web at www.WordTruthPress.com

Look for more great resources from WordTruth Press:

	Portraits of Forgiveness Finding the Inspiration and Courage to Forgive
Available now *$9.95 USD*	Like an old, frayed blanket there are many loose threads in our relationships. Issues and conflict divide us from family, friends, and innumerable people we encounter throughout life. The process of forgiveness is necessary to restore and rebuild those relationships. In this book you will find great stories of how God works in the lives of people to bring about forgiveness and reconciliation - binding up the loose threads and making relationships even stronger than before.

$9.95 USD Qty 50	**The Ten Commandments** ***Evangelism Tract (Qty 50)*** The Ten Commandments are shown on the front of this 3x5 card with a positive version of each command. On the back is a presentation of the gospel. It is printed with a glossy, color front and black-and-white back.
$9.95 USD Qty 50	**The Gospel of GRACE** ***Evangelism Tract (Qty 50)*** This attractive 3x5 card presents the good news using the word GRACE as an acrostic. Each letter represents a different aspect of God's grace at work in salvation. Glossy, color front and black-and-white back.
Available now *$12.95 USD*	**Speedy Devotions** ***Volume One – Wise Choices*** Do you have only a little time to study the Bible? Or does the Bible seem intimidating in its size and scope? Many find it hard to stay focused on long passages of Scripture. Yet the Bible is God's word for all people. And even a small amount of God's word can have a profound impact on your life. Volume 1 is about wise choices. This devotional takes you through the book of Proverbs where you learn great wisdom in small portions each day

	The Book of Mark
	Volume 1: Chapters 1-6

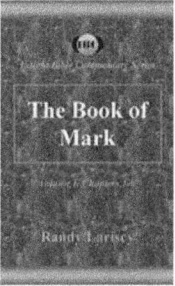

<table>
<tr>
<td></td>
<td>

The Insight Bible Commentary Series (IBC) is designed with clarity in mind. Not only will you find clear explanations of what the Bible is saying but also unique insights into how you can apply God's eternal truths to daily living. The book of Mark is generally held to be the earliest account of the life of Jesus Christ. It clearly defines its purpose in the very first verse: "The beginning of the gospel about Jesus Christ, the Son of God" (Mark 1:1, NIV). From there, the narrative presents a rapid, almost urgent look at the life of Jesus Christ. He is shown to be the Son of God with great power and authority.

</td>
</tr>
</table>

Available now

$9.95 USD

The mission of WordTruth Press is to provide quality Bible-based resources with significant spiritual impact for individuals and churches. Education and evangelism are the main focus of WordTruth Press. Following the Great Commission of the LORD Jesus (Matthew 28:18-20), this organization provides Bible-based resources to evangelize the world, encourage and equip believers and churches for evangelism, and provide solid Bible teaching to build up the body of Christ.

A key strategy is to find low-cost channels for production and distribution to maximize the availability of our resources to people around the world. WordTruth Press also offers many free resources for churches and individuals available online at:

www.WordTruthPress.com

How to Have a Personal Relationship With God

by Rev. Randy Lariscy

The most wonderful relationship you can ever have is with the One who loves you so very much that He brought you into existence. God is your Creator[2] and He desperately wants you to know Him as He knows you.[3] Can you truly say that you have a personal relationship with God? If not, these next few pages will help you to start a relationship with God that will last for time and eternity.

First, you must acknowledge that God is God and you are not. I know, you do not think you are an all-powerful being who can command things into existence. What I mean is that God is God and you do not live your life on your terms but on His terms. After all, if God is God, then He created the world in which you live. If you want to be right with God and live well in His creation, then you must submit to His rule and authority over your life.

---

[2] *In the beginning, God created the heavens and the earth. (Genesis 1:1, NIV)*

[3] *You will seek me and find me when you seek me with all your heart. (Jeremiah 29:13, NIV)*

Why does that seem so hard? From the very beginning, the first man and woman chose to live life on their own terms.[4] And every human being since has chosen the same path.[5] We want what we want when we want it - usually without regard to the consequences. The Bible calls this sin.[6] God is perfect and has a perfect standard of righteousness. When we try to live apart from God, we cross over the line of righteousness into sin. This tendency toward selfishness is part of our inner being. It is why we cannot feel right with God – because God is holy and we are not.

The good news is that God desires to have a relationship with you anyway. He has done everything necessary for you to enter into a right relationship with Him:

- God stepped out of heaven and became a real human being – without the sinful nature that we have. This is Jesus.[7]
- He lived the perfect life that you and I can never live.[8]
- Jesus offered His perfect life on a cross to pay the penalty for your sins – and for the sins of everyone in the world.[9]

---

[4] *Genesis 3:1-19. God made Adam and Eve without sin but with the ability to make choices. Each of them chose to disobey God's one command to them.*
[5] *Romans 5:12. Adam, the first man, is the father of all human beings.*
[6] *There is no difference, for all have sinned and fall short of the glory of God. (Romans 3:22-23, NIV)*
[7] *In the beginning was the Word [Jesus], and the Word was with God, and the Word was God ... The Word became flesh and made his dwelling among us. (John 1:1,14, NIV)*
[8] *God made him [Jesus] who had no sin to be a sin offering for us, so that in him we might become the righteousness of God. (2 Corinthians 5:21, NIV)*

- He rose from the dead so you can know that He is LORD, His sacrifice was acceptable, and that your sins are forgiven.[10]

If you will trust in Jesus as LORD of your life and believe His death on the cross paid for your sins, you will be forgiven and given eternal life.[11] Eternal life is not some wispy existence as an angel sitting on a cloud strumming a harp. Eternal life is a forever relationship with God that starts the moment you choose to believe.

God loves you because He created you – you belong to Him.[12] Will you accept His grace and forgiveness and enter into a loving relationship with your Creator? If this is your desire, you can pray to the LORD right now. You can use the words of this prayer to help you in this first step. The power is not in the words themselves but in your agreement with them and belief in the God who made you:

> *Dear LORD Jesus - thank You for never giving up on me. I want to have a loving relationship with You. Please forgive*

---

[9] *For Christ died for sins once for all, the righteous for the unrighteous, to bring you to God. (1 Peter 3:18, NIV)*
[10] *... for us who believe in him who raised Jesus our Lord from the dead. He was delivered over to death for our sins and was raised to life for our justification. (Romans 4:23-25, NIV)*
[11] *That if you confess with your mouth, "Jesus is Lord," and believe in your heart that God raised him from the dead, you will be saved. For it is with your heart that you believe and are justified, and it is with your mouth that you confess and are saved. (Romans 10:9-10, NIV)*
[12] *For God so loved the world that he gave his one and only Son,[Jesus] that whoever believes in him shall not perish but have eternal life. For God did not send his Son into the world to condemn the world, but to save the world through him. (John 3:16-17, NIV)*

me – not because I deserve it but because You died on a cross for my sins. Since You rose from the dead, I put my faith and trust in You and will begin to follow you because you are LORD. Thank you for giving me eternal life and hope. Amen.

If you prayed in earnest, you should be filled with the joy of knowing God and being in a right relationship with Him. The Bible says, "Yet to all who received him, to those who believed in his name, he gave the right to become children of God" (John 1:12, NIV). Welcome to God's family – forever!

www.ingramcontent.com/pod-product-compliance
Lightning Source LLC
Chambersburg PA
CBHW031316040426
42443CB00005B/97